Multidisciplinary Teamwork in Healthcare
http://dx.doi.org/10.5772/10.5772/intechopen.1002167
Edited by Neil E. Grunberg

Contributors
Abdulla Al-Ansari, Anette Fosse, Birgit Abelsen, Erin S. Barry, Habiba Arafa, Ikpoko-ore-ebirien Dike Isaruk, Kareem El-Ansari, Kaveh Same, Kirpa Chandan, Nastaran Maghbouli, Neil E. Grunberg, Richard Chivaka, Rupal Lovell-Patel, Russell Hitchen, Walid El Ansari

First published in London, United Kingdom, 2024 by IntechOpen
IntechOpen is the global imprint of INTECHOPEN LIMITED, registered in England and Wales, registration number: 11086078, 167-169 Great Portland Street, London, W1W 5PF, United Kingdom

British Library Cataloguing-in-Publication Data
A catalogue record for this book is available from the British Library

Additional hard and PDF copies can be obtained from orders@intechopen.com

Multidisciplinary Teamwork in Healthcare
Edited by Neil E. Grunberg
p. cm.

This title is part of the Business, Management and Economics Book Series, Volume 19
Topic: Business and Management
Series Editor: Taufiq Choudhry
Topic Editors: Vito Bobek and Tatjana Horvat

Print ISBN 978-0-85466-875-5
Online ISBN 978-0-85466-874-8
eBook (PDF) ISBN 978-0-85466-876-2
ISSN 2753-894X

For EU product safety concerns:
IN TECH d.o.o., Prolaz Marije Krucifikse Kozulić 3, 51000 Rijeka, Croatia,
info@intechopen.com or visit our website at intechopen.com.

IntechOpen Book Series

Business, Management and Economics

Volume 19

Aims and Scope of the Series

This series will provide a comprehensive overview of recent research trends in business and management, economics, and marketing. Topics will include asset liability management, financial consequences of the financial crisis and covid-19, financial accounting, mergers and acquisitions, management accounting, SMEs, financial markets, corporate finance and governance, managerial technology and innovation, resource management and sustainable development, social entrepreneurship, corporate responsibility, ethics and accountability, microeconomics, labour economics, macroeconomics, public economics, financial economics, econometrics, direct marketing, creative marketing, internet marketing, market planning and forecasting, brand management, market segmentation and targeting and other topics under business and management. This book series will focus on various aspects of business and management whose in-depth understanding is critical for business and company management to function effectively during this uncertain time of financial crisis, Covid-19 pandemic, and military activity in Europe.

Meet the Series Editor

Prof. Choudhry holds a BSc degree in Economics from the University of Iowa, as well as a Masters and Ph.D. in Applied Economics from Clemson University, USA. In January 2006, he became a Professor of Finance at the University of Southampton Business School. He was previously a Professor of Finance at the University of Bradford Management School. He has over 80 articles published in international finance and economics journals. His research interests and specialties include financial econometrics, financial economics, international economics and finance, housing markets, financial markets, among others.

Meet the Volume Editor

Neil E. Grunberg, Ph.D., is a medical psychologist, social psychologist, and neuroscientist. He earned a BS in medical microbiology (1975) at Stanford University and MA (1977), MPhil (1979), and Ph.D. (1980) degrees in physiological and social psychology at Columbia University. He has published more than 220 papers addressing behavioral medicine, drug use, stress, traumatic brain injury, leadership, and followership. He has been recognized by awards from the American Psychological Association, Centers for Disease Control & Prevention, Food & Drug Administration, National Cancer Institute, Society for Behavioral Medicine, U.S. Surgeon General, and Uniformed Services University. Dr. Grunberg is a U.S. Presidential Leadership Scholar, co-founder of the Healthcare Leadership Community of the International Leadership Association, and co-founder of the World Health Leadership Network.

Contents

Preface

Successful healthcare contributes to the prevention of illnesses and injuries, provides effective treatments for and rehabilitation from illnesses and injuries, and affects physical, psychological, and social health and well-being. Twenty-first-century healthcare has become a "team sport" that requires contributions, cooperation, and communication among members of multidisciplinary teams who have valuable and diverse knowledge, skills, abilities, perspectives, and wisdom. These teams include physicians, nurses, dentists, psychologists, physical and occupational therapists, and other healthcare practitioners; healthcare researchers, scholars, and educators; healthcare administrators and policymakers; as well as patients and patients' significant others.

This volume includes chapters that address multidisciplinary teamwork and relevant principles and practices of leadership and followership in healthcare from many different professional, scholarly, and experiential perspectives from experts around the globe. The chapters are written by scholars, practitioners, and educators from Canada, Grenada, Iran, Nigeria, Norway, Qatar, South Africa, United Kingdom, and the United States. It is the goal of this volume to increase understanding of what factors improve and detract from effective multidisciplinary teamwork in healthcare in order to improve its application and enhance the well-being of patients, practitioners, and all members of healthcare teams. Each chapter stands alone to make a meaningful contribution regarding multidisciplinary teamwork in healthcare. Together, the chapters form a comprehensive gestalt regarding this vital topic.

In Chapter 1, "Multidisciplinary Teamwork in the Healthcare Setting", Kaveh Same and Nastaran Maghbouli discuss relevant history and definitions regarding teams, teamwork theories and models, significance of teamwork in healthcare, teamworking skills, team challenges, and the significance of interdisciplinary teams in rehabilitation medicine. In Chapter 2, "Teamwork as Antidotes in Efficient Health Care Delivery: Challenges and Prospect of Its Implementation in Health Facilities", Ikpoko-ore-ebirien Dike Isaruk presents definitions of team and teamwork, discusses the importance of teamwork in healthcare service delivery, and challenges in effective teamwork implementation among health and allied healthcare providers. In Chapter 3, "Multidisciplinary Teamwork and Interprofessional Partnerships in Healthcare Setting: The Critical Ingredients", Walid El Ansari, Kareem El-Ansari, Habiba Arafa, and Abdulla Al-Ansari discuss the benefits of effective teamwork, challenges to effective teamwork, stages of joint working efforts, teamwork enablers, and evaluation of joint and teamworking efforts. In Chapter 4, "From a Group of People to a Well-Functioning Team: A Transformative Leadership Model in Healthcare", Richard Chivaka focuses on transforming healthcare workers into well-functioning teams, the importance of teamwork in healthcare, challenges in healthcare teamwork, components of the transformative leadership model, the team development journey, building trust, overcoming challenges in transforming healthcare worker groups into teams, evaluating the success of this transformation, and future trends and challenges. In Chapter 5, "Team Effectiveness in General Practice: Insights from the Norwegian Primary Healthcare Team Pilot", Birgit Abelsen and Anette Fosse report the results of a qualitative study of healthcare teams in five general medical practices and identify five themes relevant to team effectiveness: teamwork nature, buy-in, macro-team leadership, individual satisfaction, and performance outcome. In Chapter 6, "How to AID Leadership and Followership in Multidisciplinary Healthcare Teams", Neil E. Grunberg and Erin S. Barry discuss members of teams, team processes, leadership and followership, how to assess and develop team members, and how to optimize or "AID" multidisciplinary healthcare teamwork by applying adaptive, innovative, and distributed leadership and followership. In Chapter 7, "Perspective Chapter: Opportunities and Barriers to Effective Multidisciplinary Teamwork in the Education and Training of Allied-Healthcare Students", Kirpa Chandan, Russell Hitchen, and Rupal Lovell-Patel emphasize the importance and challenges of educating healthcare providers as multidisciplinary teams and present a head injury/concussion educational module as an example how to promote cross collaboration among healthcare professionals in higher educational settings.

I am grateful to the authors who contributed chapters to this volume as well as to our many colleagues, teachers, students, patients, friends, and family members who have encouraged and supported us in our professional and personal lives. I also am grateful to Elvira Baumgartner and the outstanding IntechOpen staff for their valuable contributions to this volume.

Neil E. Grunberg
Uniformed Services University,
Bethesda, Maryland, USA

Chapter 1

Multidisciplinary Teamwork in the Healthcare Setting

Kaveh Same and Nastaran Maghbouli

Abstract

The term "team" comes from the Proto-Germanic word "taumaz," meaning to pull and was originally used to refer to a group of yoked animals. Teams are social constructs that require a high level of interdependence in individual tasks and ongoing communication among members to achieve common goals. Different types of teams are classified based on their level of performance, with high-performing teams meeting specific criteria and demonstrating extraordinary performance and highly committed members. Various theories and approaches have been developed to understand the inner workings of effective teams, including social psychological, sociotechnical, ecological, human resources, technological, team lifecycle, task-oriented, and integrative approaches. Specific teamwork skills, such as adaptability, leadership, and effective communication, are essential for the success of a team. Assessing these skills can be challenging, as they are impacted by the specific task and team goals, leading to the need for careful and objective measurement. Developing reliable assessment tools and understanding the evolving nature of teams is crucial for accurately evaluating and improving teamwork skills. Addressing teamwork challenges requires attention to trust, clarity, conflicts, communication, and competition, with strong leadership playing a crucial role.

Keywords: team, multidisciplinary, teamwork in healthcare, team structure, teamwork challenges, team interactions

1. Introduction

Throughout the entire history of mankind, we have resorted to working together in a *team* whenever the burdens of individual tasks have seemed overwhelming or the prospects of success slim. After all, *Homo sapiens* is considered a social animal in regard with their way of life [1]. However, Cohen and Levesque argue in their 1991 paper that for a collective effort to be truly effective and hence worthy of the name 'teamwork' and the members recognized as a *team*, more is required than a number of individuals who simply follow the same set of rules and instructions even if working towards the same shared goals [2]. Contrasting between a group of cars in traffic and a convoy, they argue that while the former may follow identical traffic rules and even act coordinated and with the same goal of avoiding accidents and reaching their destination, their efforts do not constitute as true 'teamwork'. The latter on the other hand, consists of a number of cars that act as *one* in all their actions and show a certain level of *shared conventions and mental state* that Cohen et al. argue is necessary for a group effort to become *teamwork* and is in itself only achievable through *effective communication*, and ultimately leads towards all involved parties to achieve a sense of *joint intention* among themselves. The remainder of this chapter aims to dive deeper into the concept of team and teamwork and how it affects healthcare.

1.1 Definition of a team

The term *team* is derived from the Proto-Germanic *taumaz*, which means *to pull*. In Old English it was used to refer to *a set of animals yoked together*, and it was as recent as the 16th century that it first became used for humans and ultimately found the general meaning of *a group of people that are working together* [3].

Dyer defines teams as social constructs with a high degree of interdependency in individual tasks and the need for effective and continues communication among members that also poses common and valued goals [4]. Salas and others further expand on that definition by recognizing a distinction between *teamwork* that they define as the collective efforts in which involvement of more than one member of the team is required and the intermediary goals are not achievable without properly coordinated efforts of interdependent agents part of the team; and *taskwork*, which is defined in their work as all the components of the team members' actions that do not require such aforementioned interactions and are performed independent of other members [5]. Furthermore, the terms *team performance* and *team cognition* are described in their work respectively as the sum of team members' *teamwork* and *taskwork* through the entire process during which the team is active, and the collective understanding that results from the interconnected interactions of the individuals within the team. Finally, *team effectiveness* is resulted upon evaluation of the team performance based on a particular set of criteria [5].

Smith and others take a somewhat different approach and while initially provide a similar overall definition of the *team*, further define different types of teams based on their level of performance:

- *Pseudo teams* are a group of individuals that while working together actually underperform compared to their individual average.

- *Potential teams* are defined as groups that poses substantial problems in their communications and believes but non the less are able to perform slightly above individual averages.

- *Real teams* are those who achieve their expected goals and perform quite well.

- *High-performing teams* meet all the conditions of *real teams* and in addition have highly committed members and are able to perform extraordinarily and higher than expected.

It goes without saying that the goal should be for all teams to achieve the status of a *high-performing team* through effective communication and other constructive measures [6].

1.2 Teamwork theories and models

During the years, there have been numerous attempts at trying to systematically define and model the inner workings of an effective team and as Salas puts it "*how to turn a team of experts into an expert team*". Earlier approaches usually focused on the role of different inputs received by a team, e.g., the defined tasks, expected output, individual member characteristics, etc. [7, 8]. While such an approach provided valuable insight into the inner workings of a team, it seemed to overlook dynamic aspects of teamwork, i.e., how each decision and action by a team member might affect the final output of the team.

In an attempt to further investigate the teams and their innerworkings, Paris and colleagues classify eight theories or approaches that affect our understanding of how human groups function [ref-sycara-paris]:

1. Social psychological: Focusing on how team members interact and relate to one another.

2. Sociotechnical: Assessing member relations from a work and task-related standpoint.

3. Ecological: How working environments can influence teamwork.

4. Human Resources: In what way does the team utilizes its members' abilities and expertise.

5. Technological: Effect of technology on the teamwork

6. Team Lifecycle: How the team's performance changes during its lifecycle.

7. Task-oriented: How team roles relate to their functions and tasks.

8. Integrative: How a combination of the above approaches may be used together to yield a more complete picture of the team dynamic and function.

While the above-mentioned approaches are interesting and clarifying in order to create a pathway and provide us with tools that may be used to improve our understanding of *teams* and *teamwork*, it is in fact the results of such theories and approaches are shed light on the important characteristics of teamwork. To that end, the following seven principles were illustrated by Salas and others:

1. Teamwork is described by a set of dynamic and adoptive beliefs, attitudes, and actions [9].

   If defined as the sum of behaviors and actions performed by each team member with the goal of achieving a certain task, *teamwork* can then be defined as the collection of those behaviors and how they relate to each other and also to the attitudes and beliefs of each member. Such a definition while seemingly straightforward, does little in the way of providing a solid path toward actual determination of each of these characteristics in a particular team. A challenge further complicated by the everchanging nature of the team and teamwork during the entirety of their task [10]. Such complications have led some researchers to conclude that even if a fixed set of core competencies exist that will render a teamwork effective, their significance and importance will probably vary in different teams [11].

2. True teamwork requires all members to monitor other members actions and provide feedback regarding those actions [9, 12, 13].

   Such behavior monitoring can benefit teams in two major ways: It can encourage team members to always perform their best by limiting the grounds for *loafing* and can minimize the chances of mistakes by the very nature of monitoring [14].

3. Teamwork requires members to be able and willing to help other members and provide *compensatory behavior* [9].

   Considering the major advantages of a team to be the fact that they are able to work more effectively than the sum of their members' abilities, it becomes a necessity for members to be somewhat familiar with other individuals' responsibilities and areas of expertise as well as those of their own in order to be able to provide support when needed [15].

4. To be effective, teamwork requires clear and concise communication [16].

   Canon and Bowers define effective communication as a process by which clear and accurate information is exchanged between members using the proper terminology [17]. Others argue that effective communication is more than simple and free conversation and requires careful management to be effective especially as the size of the team expands [14].

5. Considering the high interdependency of individual actions within a team, teamwork requires careful coordination between members' actions [18].

   Suggested by research to be bolstered via correct implementation of the third principle discussed [13, 19], and also highly dependent on the fourth principle of effective communication, effective coordination is vital between members to avoid accidents and to help with the decision-making in cases of emergency and hardship.

6. A leadership capable of planning, setting the direction, and determination and coordination of actions [20, 21].

   Determining each member's task, coordinating activities, and creating effective communication between the members are crucial leadership responsibilities that greatly affect the efficiency of the teamwork.

7. Exact characteristics of the teamwork are determined by the requirements of the task [17].

While general principles and characteristics are discussed here that are important for the effectiveness of the teamwork, it is once again emphasized that the nature of the task and structure of the team determine the exact qualities expected of the team [17].

2. Significance of teamwork in healthcare

Having found a basic understanding of what is considered true teamwork and how effective teams tend to function, we now turn towards the use and significance of teamwork in healthcare. In the following lines, examples of how real teamwork can improve the patient outcome or even prove lifesaving, are discussed in detail.

The vitality of teamwork can perhaps be best understood in the care of the surgical patient in the operating room (OR). The complex and high stakes conditions command the implementation of a highly efficient team in order to be able to face the challenges and properly respond to emergency situations. With the OR team comprising of anesthesiologists, nurses, surgeons, and sometimes other operation-specific specialists, stablishing effective communication between team members is vital. Watkins et al. state that more than two-thirds of all failures related to the OR occur as a result of errors in communication rather than technical failures [22]. Such results emphasize the role of careful assessment in order for the policymaking bodies to identify and address problems.

In a review by Slowey and Abernathy, the effect of team and teamwork was assessed in the care of thoracic surgery patients. Classifying the team dynamics present in the thoracic OR into four dyads (namely the surgeon–nurse, surgeon–trainee, anesthesiologist–nurse, and surgeon–anesthesiologist). While reviewing the literature, they found that previous collaboration between within each dyad plays a significantly more important role than individual experience of team members. Furthermore, they identified five main characteristics (the "*Big five*"), that greatly influence the effectiveness of the team and roots of many failures can be traced back to malfunctions in one or more of these characteristics [23]:

- Team leadership: Ability to coordinate and direct member actions.
- Mutual performance monitoring: Ability to accurately understand and monitor each team member's performance.
- Backup behavior: Ability to understand team member needs and responsibilities with the goal of providing support or workload shifts among members when needed.
- Adaptability: Ability to adjust strategy based on the current team and task state.
- Team orientation: Believing in the importance of team goals and their precedence over individual goals.

Recognizing the importance of leadership as one of the most important characteristics of an effective team, Rosenman et al. conducted a narrative review in order to further assess the quality of team leadership education in the setting of emergency medicine (EM) and suggest ways in which resident competencies can be evaluated in this regard [24]. Current standard evaluations regarding teamwork in EM residents include a milestone program that assesses individual resident's team management skills in a five-step manner in which the first milestone corresponds to the level expected of an intern and the fifth to those of an experienced physician. The residents are expected to reach step four during their training. Rosenman and her team devised a similar milestone assessment tool that focused on leadership skills with steps ranging from the individual having the ability to ask for help when needed and being able to treat others with respect in the first step, all the way to having the ability to effectively managing team resources, motivating members, and resolving conflicts [24]. Such innovations need further investigation regarding effective ways of teamwork education in healthcare workers as well as practical tools for assessment of such skills.

Focusing on another branch of medicine, Fernando and Hughes reviewed the importance of teamwork in the palliative care of terminally ill patients. A vast field requiring coordination between many specialists, palliative care is usually a group effort in many corners of the world. However, in the absence of a standardized approach to the management and structure of such a team, they found significant variation between the structure, efficiency, and working principles of the healthcare team around the globe. Contrasting between multi-disciplinary, inter-disciplinary, and trans-disciplinary when applied to a team, they state the best structure for a healthcare team active in the field of palliative medicine is to be *inter-disciplinary* meaning that there should exist a meaningful amount of overlap in each team member's responsibilities and their understanding of other members' role in the team to allow support and synergy between members in the group to take place. Such a team, in conjunction with an effective communication and strong leadership, will be ideal for administration of palliative care to the patients [25].

3. Teamworking skills: from challenges to resolution

So far, we have discussed the general principles and characteristics that make up an effective team. Though somewhat similar in nature to the aforementioned characteristics, we will now focus on the skills that each member of a team should have in order to properly achieve the collective goals of the team, as well as methods available for the assessment of such skills. Next, we shall have a look on the challenges faced by a team and ways for overcoming those challenges and conflicts.

3.1 Teamwork skills

As mentioned previously, researchers believe that defining a set of skills that if available will result in the formation of the ideal team is somewhat problematic as many of the required skill will either completely change or at least vary in their importance depending on the exact task and team goals. Nonetheless, to circumvent this issue to some degree, Salas and others have tried to classify different skills exactly based on their dependence on a particular task or team (whether each skill or its importance is dependent on a specific task or team or can be considered universal) [17, 26]. Skills are summarized in **Table 1**. Note that many skills may appear more than once as they may be thought of to be required in more than one level.

Nature of skill	Skills
Team Generic Task Generic	• Morale building • Challenge resolution • Effective communication • Task motivation • Co-operation • Consulting • Confidence
Team Specific Task Generic	• Challenge resolution • Motivation promotion • Effective communication • Intra-team feedback • Backup behavior • Confidence • Planning Flexibility • Morale building • Co-operation
Team Generic Task Specific	• Task structuring • Mission analysis • Task sequencing • Mutual performance monitoring • Backup behavior • Effective communication • Intra-team feedback • Confidence • Flexibility • Planning • Task interaction • Situational awareness
Team Specific Task Specific	• Task organization • Mutual performance monitoring • Shared problem-model development • Flexibility • Backup behavior • Effective communication • Dynamic reallocation of functions • Task structuring • Task interaction • Motivation promotion

Table 1.
Skills required by an ideal team classified based on the task/team specificity/genericity.

3.2 How to assess teamwork skills

The need for careful and objective measurement of teamwork skills within a team are essential for the team to be able to improve their functions and more efficiently move towards their goals. As such, due to the nature of the many necessary skills required by a team, for such an assessment to be objective and not affected by rater bias is no easy task. Indeed, most if not all the measurement tools depend on rater's decision to score each skill.

Some of the earliest works in this regard were those by Schiflett and colleagues in which core competencies expected in a team were observed in the team's behavior and rated using checklists [27]. Despite their dependence on examiner decision, their method was shown to have acceptable inter-rater reliability. In another effort, Morgen and others developed the Critical Team Behaviors Form (CTBF) in 1986. The CTBF again used rating team members' behavior by completing a checklist covering critical team behaviors classified into seven categories [28].

In their review of the teamwork measurement methods, Baker et al. concluded that while actual methods used in the assessment of a team may be greatly varied (and more often than not, rather inaccurate!), by following a series of principles, one may be able to design an effective and reliable means of assessing teamworking skills in a particular team. These principles are as follows [29]:

1. If one is to truly understand the innerworkings of a team, a good and robust theory of how teams' function is the way to go.

2. As teams evolve in their needs and functions with time, assessments must also be dynamic and repeated through time.

3. There seem to be no way to avoid the need for observation when measuring team skills. Therefore, care must be taken in the development of measurement methods to maximize inter-rater agreement.

4. A main point of focus should be to try and assess wide variations of teams as possible. Only through rigorous assessment attempt can we streamline our assessment tools and find solutions for unanswered questions.

5. Reliability and stability of assessment tools must be investigated both from an inter-rater agreement and also temporally.

6. Care must be taken to ensure validity of the measurement construct. Pursuing a multimodal approach in the design of the assessment tool, as well as factor analysis, may prove rewarding paths to follow.

Focusing more on the teams active in healthcare, an interesting observation regarding team performance assessment was the fact that self-assessments tended to be quite inaccurate and unreliable, with physicians constantly reporting higher scores compared to nurses [22], thus emphasizing the need for more sophisticated measures. Two of the tools designed to measure team performance in multi-disciplinary surgical teams are the Observational Teamwork Assessment for Surgery (OTAS) [30] and Revised Oxford Nontechnical Skills (NOTECHS) scale [31]. While the former assesses team performance in five categories (namely collaboration, coordination, teamwork, communication, and situational awareness), the NOTECHS measures nontechnical skills in four dimensions of cooperation, leadership, decision-making, and situational awareness. As our understanding of how teams function evolves, so does our tools for the measurement of their skills and performance.

3.3 Challenges in the team and how to solve them

Working in a team, especially in healthcare setting, is challenging. Suppose stressful environment of an emergency room with irrefutable role of team working in patients' management who are struggling for life. Inattention to these challenges causes loss of productivity and inspiring atmosphere in work place. Here, we will discuss some challenges teams face commonly and the ways to untie them.

3.3.1 Trust

If we analogize a relationship to a building, trust is its core block. Lack of trust causes demotivation among team members. Trust is a key component of a relationship and needs enough time to exist and persist. Paying attention to trust formation between team members especially in first days is the most important point in team formation. Trust issues in teamwork can arise when team members doubt each other's intentions, capabilities, or reliability. These issues can stem from past experiences of being let down or betrayed by team members, leading to a lack of confidence in their ability to contribute effectively to the team. Trust is essential for a team to work cohesively and productively, as it fosters open communication, collaboration, and a sense of accountability among team members. Without trust, team members may struggle to rely on each other, leading to conflicts, misunderstandings, and ultimately hindering the team's ability to achieve its goals. Building and maintaining trust within a team requires consistent communication, mutual respect, and a commitment to transparency and reliability.

Clearly defining roles, responsibilities, and goals for each team member to ensure everyone is on the same page can help in trust issues resolution. Establishing clear expectations will help build trust as team members know what is expected of them and how their contributions fit into the larger team goals. Encouraging ownership of tasks and responsibilities is another way to build trust within the team. By holding team members accountable, you show that you value their contributions and trust them to deliver on their commitments. Building relationships and rapport with team members can help create a sense of trust and camaraderie within the team. Consider hosting team-building activities or social events to foster stronger relationships among team members [32].

3.3.2 Clarity

Clarity issues in teamwork can arise when there is a lack of clear communication, goals, and roles within the team. This can lead to confusion, misunderstandings, and disagreements among team members. Without clear direction and expectations, individuals may struggle to understand their responsibilities and how they contribute to the overall team goals. Additionally, ambiguous communication can result in poor decision-making and a lack of alignment within the team. To address clarity issues, it is important for team leaders to provide clear guidance, establish open communication channels, and regularly check in with team members to ensure everyone is on the same page. By promoting transparency and clarity within the team, members can work effectively towards common goals and achieve success.

Clearly defining each team member's role and responsibilities can help prevent confusion and ensure that everyone knows what is expected of them. Establishing effective communication channels, such as regular team meetings, email updates, and project management tools, can help ensure that team members are on the same page and can easily share information. Open and honest communication within the team can help prevent misunderstandings and promote collaboration. Regularly providing feedback to team members on their performance and contributions can help address any clarity issues and ensure that everyone is aligned with the team's goals. Using visual aids, such as charts, diagrams, and project timelines, can help clarify complex concepts and make it easier for team members to understand their roles and responsibilities. Encouraging team members to actively listen to each other can help prevent misunderstandings and ensure that everyone is on the same page. Sometimes, we need training. Providing training and development opportunities for team members can help improve their skills and knowledge, leading to better collaboration and clarity within the team.

3.3.3 Conflicts

Conflicts in teamwork arise when team members have differing opinions, personalities, or work styles that clash with one another. These conflicts can be caused by misunderstandings, miscommunication, or simply by the stress of working together towards a shared goal. Conflict can also be indicative of deeper underlying issues within the team, such as lack of trust, poor leadership, or unequal distribution of work. If not addressed, conflicts can lead to decreased productivity, morale, and cohesiveness among team members. However, when managed effectively, conflicts can actually lead to better solutions and stronger teamwork. It is important for team members to openly communicate, listen to each other's perspectives, and work towards a resolution that benefits the team as a whole.

To identify root causes, we should work together as a team to identify the underlying issues that are causing the conflict. This could involve uncovering miscommunication, misunderstandings, or differing expectations. Once the root cause is identified, working together to come up with a solution that addresses the conflict in a constructive and mutually beneficial way is an effective method. If the conflict persists or escalates, engaging a neutral third party is a wise option to help facilitate a resolution. In addition, setting clear guidelines and norms for communication and conflict resolution within the team is beneficial to help prevent future conflicts from arising.

3.3.4 Communication

When team members do not effectively communicate with each other, it can lead to misunderstandings, delays in project completion, and conflicts within the team. Some common communication issues include unclear communication, lack of active listening, and differences in communication styles. Unclear communication can result in team members not understanding tasks or expectations, leading to confusion and mistakes. Additionally, when team members do not actively listen to each other, important information can be missed or misinterpreted. Furthermore, differences in communication styles, such as one team member preferring face-to-face communication while another prefers emails, can lead to misunderstandings and miscommunication. To overcome communication issues, it is important for teams to establish clear communication channels, actively listen to one another, and be open to understanding and respecting each other's communication preferences.

Communication issues in teamwork can be resolved by establishing clear and open channels of communication. This involves setting clear expectations and objectives for each team member, encouraging feedback and active listening, and promoting transparency in sharing information. Regular team meetings and updates can also help to ensure that everyone is on the same page and aligned towards common goals. Additionally, fostering a culture of trust and respect within the team can help to address any underlying issues and facilitate effective communication. By addressing these communication barriers proactively and creating a supportive and collaborative environment, teams can work together more efficiently and effectively towards achieving their objectives [33].

3.3.5 Competition

Competition issues in teamwork can arise when team members are more focused on outperforming each other than collaborating towards a common goal. This can lead to a lack of communication, trust, and cooperation within the team, ultimately hindering the overall productivity and success of the group. Competition can also create tension and conflict among team members, leading to a toxic work environment and decreased morale. It is important for team leaders to foster a culture of collaboration, mutual respect, and shared goals to mitigate competition issues and ensure the team's effectiveness and cohesion [34]. Encouraging open communication, promoting teamwork, and acknowledging and rewarding collective achievements are key strategies to address competition issues in teamwork.

Competition issues in teamwork can often arise due to conflicting interests, lack of communication, and differing personal goals. In order to address these issues, it is important for team members to establish clear expectations and goals from the outset. Communication also plays a crucial role in resolving competition issues, as it allows team members to openly discuss their concerns and work towards finding a mutually beneficial solution. Additionally, fostering a sense of trust and collaboration within the team can help to minimize the negative effects of competition and promote a more harmonious working environment. Ultimately, by fostering a strong sense of unity and common purpose, team members can overcome competition issues and work together towards achieving shared goals.

As conclusion, all challenges influence each other and to control each one, focusing on all challenges is necessary. Strong leadership is essential in effectively resolving teamwork challenges and promoting a culture of teamwork and collaboration within an organization. Good leaders not only provide support and empowerment for team members but also help in conflict resolution and decision makings.

4. Significance of inter-disciplinary teams in rehabilitation medicine

In this part, we will explain a successful teamwork experience in managing patients in the form of a multidisciplinary team. This team consists of an orthopedic surgeon, a neurologist, a physical medicine and rehabilitation specialist, an orthotic and prosthesis specialist, and a neurosurgeon. Complex patients who require multidisciplinary care are referred to this interdisciplinary clinic. Patients are visited simultaneously by doctors from the mentioned specialized fields. Then, each specialist presents his opinion about the management of the patient from the point of view of his specialized field, and the final treatment plan of the patient is decided by team consensus. Each doctor has the opportunity to examine the patient, and other doctors also can see important points in the history and examination of the patient from the view of each specialty. During the 3 years since the establishment of this weekly clinic, more than 800 patients have been treated and rehabilitated in this setting.

One of the important points in the success of this clinic is the strong leadership of this program in such a way that all team members follow the group leader and have enough trust in him. The goals of this clinic are clear to all team members and participants know exactly what they will achieve from this program. The roles and responsibilities of each person are clearly defined. For example, if a patient needs Botox injections to manage spasticity, this work is done by a neurologist and all members know and accept this work allocation. Leader's expectations are clear and explained to all members at the beginning of the program. Each team member is trusted and have responsibilities, and no one is ignored. The members of this team have a virtual group for coordination and follow-up of patients and discussion about patients, in which they exchange opinions during the week in addition to the day they attend the clinic. The team leader gives regular feedback to the team members about their contribution and function. For example, if any of the members do not participate in several sessions or do not provide the results of the follow-up of the patient, they will be questioned, while if there is a personal problem that is preventing them from performing responsibilities related to the clinic, they will be supported by other team members. Active listening to team members is one of the characteristics of the team leader and team members that causes effective relationships among people. Conflicts among team members have been resolved by talking and expressing expectations, and if the problem persists, the team leader and sometimes a person from outside the team are invited to judge. The culture of teamwork and collective decision-making caused lack of toxic competitive atmosphere in this team and everyone does their best towards achieving common goals.

5. Conclusion

Working in a team, especially in a healthcare setting, can be challenging. It is important to address these challenges in order to maintain productivity and a positive work environment. Trust is a key component in team dynamics and should be established early on. Clearly defining roles and expectations, as well as promoting transparency and effective communication, can help ensure that everyone is on the same page and working towards common goals. Strong leadership is key to effectively resolving these challenges and promoting a culture of teamwork and collaboration.

Author details

Kaveh Same[1] and Nastaran Maghbouli[2]*

1 Center for Orthopedic Trans-disciplinary Applied Research (COTAR), Tehran University of Medical Sciences, Tehran, Iran

2 Department of Physical Medicine and Rehabilitation, School of Medicine, Tehran University of Medical Sciences, Tehran, Iran

*Address all correspondence to: nmaghbouli@sina.tums.ac.ir

References

[1] Tomasello M. The ultra-social animal. European Journal of Social Psychology. 2014;**44**(3):187-194

[2] Cohen PR, Levesque HJ. Teamwork. Nous. 1991;**25**(4):487-512

[3] Dictionary OE. Oxford English Dictionary. Simpson, Ja & Weiner, Esc; 1989. p. 3

[4] Dyer JL. Team research and team training: A state-of-the-art review. Human Factors Review. 1984;**26**:285-323

[5] Salas E, Cooke NJ, Rosen MA. On teams, teamwork, and team performance: Discoveries and developments. Human Factors. 2008;**50**(3):540-547

[6] Smith KA, Imbrie P. Teamwork and Project Management. University of Minnesota. McGraw-Hill; 2004

[7] Goldstein IL. Training in Organizations: Needs Assessment, Development, and Evaluation. Thomson Brooks/Cole Publishing Co.; 1993

[8] Campion MA, Medsker GJ, Higgs AC. Relations between work group characteristics and effectiveness: Implications for designing effective work groups. Personnel Psychology. 1993;**46**(4):823-847

[9] McIntyre RM, Salas E. Measuring and managing for team performance: Emerging principles from complex environments. Team Effectiveness and Decision Making in Organizations. 1995;**16**:9-45

[10] Serfaty D, Entin EE, Johnston JH. Team coordination training. In: Cannon-Bowers JA, Salas E, editors. Making Decisions Under Stress: Implications for Individual and Team Training. American Psychological Association; 1998. pp. 221-245

[11] Salas E, Cannon-Bowers J. The Anatomy of Team Training. Training and Retraining: A Handbook for Business, Industry, Government, and the Military; 2000. pp. 312-335

[12] Smith-Jentsch KA, Salas E, Baker DP. Training team performance-related assertiveness. Personnel Psychology. 1996;**49**(4):909-936

[13] Wiener EL. Crew coordination and training in the advanced-technology cockpit. In: Wiener EL, Kanki BG, Helmreich RL, editors. Cockpit Resource Management. Academic Press; 1993. pp. 199-229

[14] Stevens MJ, Campion MA. The knowledge, skill, and ability requirements for teamwork: Implications for human resource management. Journal of Management. 1994;**20**(2):503-530

[15] Briggs G, Johnston W. Team Training (NTDC Technical Report No. 1327-4). Orlando: Naval Training Device Center; 1967

[16] Kanki BG. Communication and crew resource management. In: Crew Resource Management. Academic Press; 2019. pp. 103-137

[17] Cannon-Bowers JA et al. Defining competencies and establishing team training requirements. Team Effectiveness and Decision Making in Organizations. 1995;**333**:380

[18] Kleinman DL, Serfaty D. Team performance assessment in distributed decision making. In: Proceedings of the

Symposium on Interactive Networked Simulation for Training. FL: University of Central Florida Orlando; 1989

[19] Foushee HC. Dyads and triads at 35,000 feet: Factors affecting group process and aircrew performance. American Psychologist. 1984;**39**(8):885

[20] Ginnett R. Crews as Groups: Their Formation and their Leadership. New York: Academic Press; 1993. pp. 71-98

[21] Hackman JR. Groups that work (and those that don't): Creating conditions for effective teamwork. Journal of Policy Analysis and Management. 1990

[22] Watkins SC, Hensley NB. Team dynamics in the operating room: How is team performance optimized? Anesthesiology Clinics. 2023;**41**(4):775-787

[23] Slowey C, Abernathy J. Team-based care of the thoracic surgical patient. Current Opinion in Anaesthesiology. 2024;**37**(1):79-85

[24] Rosenman ED, Branzetti JB, Fernandez R. Assessing team leadership in emergency medicine: The milestones and beyond. Journal of Graduate Medical Education. 2016;**8**(3):332-340

[25] Fernando G, Hughes S. Team approaches in palliative care: A review of the literature. International Journal of Palliative Nursing. 2019;**25**(9):444-451

[26] Salas E, Burke CS, Cannon-Bowers JA. Teamwork: Emerging principles. International Journal of Management Reviews. 2000;**2**(4):339-356

[27] Shiflett S et al. The Definition and Measurement of Small Military Unit Team Functions. Final Report, July 1980-October 1981. Bethesda, MD: Advanced Research Resources Organization; 1985

[28] Morgan Jr, BB. Measurement of Team Behaviors in a Navy Environment. Final Report. Norfolk, VA: Old Dominion University, Center for Applied Psychological Studies; 1986

[29] Baker DP, Salas E. Principles for measuring teamwork skills. Human Factors. 1992;**34**(4):469-475

[30] Undre S et al. Observational teamwork assessment for surgery (OTAS): Refinement and application in urological surgery. World Journal of Surgery. 2007;**31**:1373-1381

[31] Mishra A, Catchpole K, McCulloch P. The Oxford NOTECHS system: Reliability and validity of a tool for measuring teamwork behaviour in the operating theatre. BMJ Quality & Safety. 2009;**18**(2):104-108

[32] Burchard MA, Grunberg NE, Barry ES. Toward understanding and building trust for practicing and emerging healthcare professionals: The ASC-DOC trust model. MedEdPublish. 2020;**9**:280

[33] Ratna H. The importance of effective communication in healthcare practice. Harvard Public Health Review. 2019;**23**:1-6

[34] Swensen S, Shanafelt T. Cultivating Leadership. AMA Steps Forward; 2020

Chapter 2

Teamwork as Antidotes in Efficient Health Care Delivery: Challenges and Prospect of Its Implementation in Health Facilities

Ikpoko-ore-ebirien Dike Isaruk

Abstract

A variety of actors, including both providers and recipients, are involved in the delivery of health care services. In particular, teams from many health and related fields work together to guarantee patient happiness and quality. Nonetheless, there is a dearth of research on teamwork and difficulties in healthcare settings, and most patients frequently lament about subpar service delivery and the difficulties they have receiving care from physicians in most medical facilities. Thus, using systematic reviews of relevant literature, this research evaluated teamwork as an antidote to efficient health care delivery: challenges as well as possibilities of its application in health facilities. According to the report, effective teamwork increases satisfaction, creativity, productivity, and engagement. Working as a team improves motivation, lowers stress, promotes learning, stimulates creativity, and encourages taking risks. Open communication and mutual support contribute to increased job satisfaction, enhancing retention rates. The paper suggests that training and retraining of employees, the provision of enabling policies and environments, funding, and leadership structure should be targeted towards quality care and stakeholder involvement in ensuring satisfactory service delivery.

Keywords: antidotes, challenges, health care delivery, prospect, teamwork

1. Introduction

Health care service delivery is a multifaceted sector that necessitates a diverse group of health and allied health professionals, as well as representatives from other stakeholders and partner agencies, working as a team with the necessary knowledge and abilities to navigate holistically into the client, sick person, or group of sick people in order to ensure their health care needs satisfaction and the safety of humanity and the environment in general. In a health care setting, teamwork is a dynamic process involving two or more people, specifically health care professionals with diverse skill sets who collaborate with the sharing of objectives and physical and mental efforts in assessing, planning, and evaluating patient care.

In addition, the delivery of health care is unquestionably a team effort, and nobody can finish the health care supply chain by themselves. More than teams in other industries, medical and paramedical care teams, particularly in the dynamic domains of health care like health records outpatient units, operating rooms, intensive care, accident and emergency sections, or trauma and resuscitation teams, work under conditions that change frequently, may require leaders assembled on-the-fly, have a dynamically changing team membership, always collaborate for a brief period of time, consist of specialists or several specialist maintenance personnel, and have to integrate divergent perspectives.

Furthermore, delivering health care services involves a number of team types and formations and is intrinsically interrelated and multidimensional. To ensure high-quality patient care, teamwork in the health care industry entails a variety of professional positions arranged into various frameworks. Inter-professional practice-based approaches can enhance health care outcomes and procedures. It takes a diverse group of experts to work as a team in public health care institutions, including nurses, doctors, pharmacists, health information management specialists, and scientists and technicians from medical labs. Therefore, for the tenacity of enhancing quality health care services and delivering safe and effective care, health care providers and other employees of the health care facility must work effectively as a team.

2. Origin of teamwork

The Bible is where teamwork first appeared. The creator and implementer for teamwork is none other than God Almighty. God said to man, "Let us make man in our image, after our likeness," according to Ref. ([1], p. 26) in the Bible. He also gave him dominion over cattle, animals, fish in the sea, and all creeping things that crawl on the ground. This suggests that without teamwork, an individual cannot accomplish much. Ref. [2] states that in a different realm, two people are preferable to one as they get a high return on their effort. One of them can assist the other in getting back up if they fall. However, feel sorry for anyone who trips and falls and cannot get aid. Moreover, two will remain warm if they lie down together. But how can one survive on their own? Two can hold their own even if one is overwhelmed. A cord with three strands also does not break easily. How good and pleasant it is when God's people live together in unity, according to Ref. [3].

In addition, Ref. [4] says that as iron sharpens iron, so one person sharpens another. This implies that a team is often made up of more than one person or individual, and to work as a team, the people involved must work together and share ideas and relevant resources for the goals to be achieved. This is also exemplified in Ref. [5] which says, I appeal to you, brothers and sisters, in the name of our Lord Jesus Christ, that all of you agree with one another in what you say and that there be no divisions among you, but that you be perfectly united in mind and thought, according to Ref. [5]. Equally, in Ref. [6], the scripture says, let us consider how we may spur one another on towards love and good deeds, not giving up meeting together, as some are in the habit of doing, but encouraging one another—and all the more as you see the day approaching.

In a healthcare setting, it might be believed that Florence Nightingale and her team of nurses, dispatched by the British government in 1854 to assist in providing health care services for the soldiers, are the forerunners of teamwork. Nightingale, 1863, cited in Ref. [7], says that in 1854, Russians were forced to evacuate the Turkish provinces of Moldavia and Wallachia by British forces fighting in Crimea and the surrounding area. The British government dispatched a team of nurses to accompany Florence Nightingale to Turkey in order to assist in providing medical care for the soldiers, as cholera and diarrhoea were the main causes of death for the British soldiers. After Florence Nightingale arrived, the disease-related death rate decreased from 42 to 2.2%.

3. Definition of team and teamwork

Teams, according to Ref. [8], are made up of two or more people that collaborate to accomplish particular, shared goals, have specialised roles and task-specific competences, use resources that are available to all team members, and communicate to plan activities and adjust to change. Ref. [9] established that a team is a distinguishable group of two or more individuals who interact dynamically, dependably, and adaptively in order to achieve a shared and valued goal, who have been given specific roles or functions to carry out, and who have a finite amount of time to be a part of the team. Teamwork is the activity of amicably working well together as a team. The sixth edition of the Ref. [10] defines "teamwork" as the act of cooperating effectively as a group. Working as a team is known as teamwork, and it is defined by shared decision-making, open communication, and interdependent collaboration.

Teamwork, according to Ref. [11], entails the formation of team members, team members' relationships, team leadership, team problem solving, and organisational environment in ensuring the delivery of quality health care service to beneficiaries, either from a particular healthcare facility, level of healthcare system, or from a global collaborative perspective, with the main objective of ensuring the safety of mankind, his healthiness, and his environment. Ref. [12] averred that the variety of professional and non-professional providers involved in the delivery and organisation of health care services is becoming increasingly indicative of these services, with each team having its own area of expertise, set of responsibilities, and hierarchy within medicine and other disciplines.

As a result, ideas of "teams" in the health care industry and "teamwork" are frequently mentioned in discourses about modernising and improving the system. Teams have the potential to improve clinical care, according to Ref. [13], because they can pool, modify, combine, and apply a wider range of knowledge to make decisions, find solutions to issues, come up with new ideas, and carry out tasks more quickly and effectively than an individual working alone. Because of this potential, a diverse team of healthcare experts might ideally collaborate to make diagnoses, create care plans, carry out treatments, offer suitable follow-up, and overall serve patients with high-quality care.

4. Conceptual review of teamwork

Teamwork is crucial for delivering high-quality healthcare services. In health care delivery settings, teamwork involves collaboration among a multidisciplinary group of allied and health care providers, administrative staff, patients, and other stakeholders. Team members have a significant impact on the effectiveness of teamwork in the delivery of quality health care in hospitals. A strong health care team relationship facilitates cooperation and provides greater opportunities to share ideas, innovate, and also learn about a patient's unique health needs. More so, team relationships impact the effectiveness of teamwork in health care delivery by positively influencing patient satisfaction, employee performance, job satisfaction, and reducing costs. Team relationships also impact the effectiveness of teamwork in health care delivery, with proximity between healthcare workers facilitating trust-building and communication. According to Ref. [14], team relationships are essential for effective teamwork in delivering quality health care in hospitals. Equally, team relationships impact the effectiveness of teamwork in the delivery of quality health care by influencing the care provided and job satisfaction among health care workers.

Another development was the finding by Ref. [15] that 15% of the causes of adverse events directly relate to communication issues between health care professionals and patients or within the teams of health care professionals. In more than 50% of the cases, the incident was caused by a lack of effective teamwork. Communication failures are the leading causes of inadvertent patient harm. According to the Joint Commission for Hospital Accreditation report of analysis of 2455 sentinel events, the primary root cause in over 70% of them was communication failure. Reflecting the seriousness of these occurrences, approximately 75% of these patients died, and all too often, clinicians providing care had very different ideas about what should happen [16]. Effective communication and teamwork are aimed at creating a common mental model or getting everyone in the same picture. Equally important is creating an environment that feels safe for team members, so they will speak up when they have safety concerns. The mantra of everyone in the same picture, no surprises, is an effective one that is easy to communicate.

Although healthcare services are delivered by multiple team members, healthcare service quality and safety have historically been structured on the performance of professionals, individual practitioners, and allied health personnel. Consequently, effective communication encourages collaboration, patient safety, and a better result. Coordination, efficiency, and quality of service are critical in the operating room as a whole. These factors aid leaders in navigating effectively and efficiently to ensure team members cooperate, brainstorm, innovate, share responsibilities, and work dependently and interdependently to achieve organisational goals. In every healthcare facility, successful leadership and teamwork are lubricated by excellent communication. This allows for the delivery of high-quality healthcare services. In addition, a unified mental model, a safe atmosphere, and team members cooperating, brainstorming, innovating, and sharing duties, as well as working together and cooperatively to achieve organisational goals, are the aims of effective communication in a team relationship. This enables the provision of top-notch health care services through good team leadership.

Leadership is crucial in making it obvious that the culture demands that everyone be treated with respect on a daily basis. There is a tonne of information showing that rude, aggressive behaviour is exceedingly dangerous in the healthcare industry [17]. Universally, in an organisation, operational teamwork emerges naturally when the leaders are motivating, respectful of others' perspectives and rights, and demonstrating a lifestyle that is admirable. It is the responsibility of the leaders to convey how important it is for their teammates' efforts to contribute to the organisation's success. Higher levels of interest and dedication result when an employee's work is seen as meaningful and significant.

According to Ref. [18], leaders are crucial in encouraging team members' dedication to achieving corporate goals. Leaders who score highly in the job and support behaviour are particularly helpful at encouraging good teamwork performance. Leaders are people who develop standards and values inside an organisation while also distributing resources to colleagues to increase their availability. In addition, delegation or giving them difficult jobs that provide them some autonomy, control, performance feedback, and the chance to participate in decision-making processes also helps them develop commitment. Also, the team leader can raise team motivation by restructuring tasks to add more crucial job resources. Work resources are the social, physical, and organisational facets of the workplace that support the achievement of corporate objectives and promote individual development through delegation of functions.

According to Ref. [19], effective leadership in the field of health care has attracted research attention over the last few years, and one of the key areas of focus by the Cameroon government, which is believed to improve the country's health care sector, has been the quality of leadership. In addition, claims have been made that the most effective way of achieving high-quality service delivery would be through strong leadership. Warri further stated that the strength of the leadership within an organisation is often linked to the type of leadership style adopted by the organisation. In addition, Ref. [20] argues that team leaders can also increase team motivation by delegating work and reorganising priorities to include more essential job resources. Delegation is the act of providing someone else with work or obligations that would otherwise be yours. It is frequently required when a team leader needs additional work completed quickly and by individuals with the required technical knowledge. It is a three-way process that involves the delegation of authority by the leader, the delegation of responsibility, and the creation of accountability for subordinate acceptance or compliance [21].

5. Importance of teamwork in health care service delivery

Teamwork lowers medical errors, boosts patient safety, lessens burnout, and boosts patient happiness [22, 23]. Additionally, it decreases workloads, improves job satisfaction and retention, lowers morbidity, lowers care costs and wastages, develops spaces for professional and technical knowledge acquisition and sharing, prevents work redoing, and promotes sustainability of care consistency. Understanding teamwork helps a multifaceted health care professional's ability to debate with stakeholders. The following are some crucial grounds for implementing cooperation in health care organisations and other institutions:

Teamwork enables teams to self-monitor, evaluate, and rely on one another's work, create an avenue for efficient work, learn from each other's strengths and failures, innovate more quickly, and reduce stress. It is one of the 14 crucial elements of management principles identified by Henry Fayol and can lead to better productivity, reduced costs, greater profitability, and many other benefits [24]. Collaboration can result in more effective issue solving, faster work completion, and thorough creativity. Teamwork encourages healthy competition because employees may learn from one another and develop an environment that supports delivering high-quality health care services. Successful cooperation depends on having good working relationships and rapport, since these things can result in friendships, dependability, and attractiveness. To guarantee patient safety and high-quality health care service delivery, health care and allied health care providers must collaborate, support, and communicate effectively with one another [25].

For the purpose of providing high-quality health care, communication and teamwork skills are crucial because they can improve patient outcomes, prevent medical errors, increase efficiency, and increase patient satisfaction. A culture of learning and continuous improvement will be fostered, staff wellness will increase, patient safety will be improved, and better teamwork and communication will ensure that everyone feels empowered to voice their concerns and ask questions. Moreover, Ref. [26] assert that when co-morbidities and complexity rise and the need for high-quality patient care rises, cooperation is crucial for providing high-quality health care services.

The following are some examples of the importance of teamwork implementation in a health care setting:

1. Effective communication is fostered by teamwork.

2. Collaborating enhances idea generation.

3. A shared objective is fostered through teamwork.

4. Problem-solving abilities are enhanced in the workplace by teamwork.

5. Trust is developed through teamwork.

6. Company culture is enhanced through teamwork.

7. Efficiency is produced through teamwork.

More so, good teamwork boosts engagement, productivity, creativity, and satisfaction. Teamwork increases motivation, reduces stress, encourages learning, fosters creativity, encourages risk-taking, builds problem-solving skills, improves job satisfaction, and ensures team members feel valued. Open communication and mutual support contribute to increased job satisfaction, enhancing retention rates.

6. Challenges in effective teamwork implementation

How easily normal and non-routine day services are provided varies depending on the initiatives, interests, and personalities of different individuals in any organisation, but especially at a federal tertiary healthcare facility. In general, team members should master soft skills, including effective communication and relationship building, to enhance both individual and team performance as well as patient safety. Ref. [27] assert that the following issues prevent teamwork among health and allied healthcare providers:

In the health care sector, culture and ethnicity can be obstacles to collaboration, particularly in poor and emerging countries. This may result in difficulties with language, comprehension, and communication, as well as ineffective team leaders and bad leadership techniques. Inadequate team members or bad team formation can result from changing roles, and changing circumstances can cause teams to be formed or modified, as well as new teams to be formed or existing ones to be changed. These abilities are necessary for a team leader to successfully manage or lead a team and create a productive workplace.

Globally, diverse scholars, including Ref. [27], have established that health care service delivery is a multidisciplinary and multitasking setting involving different professionals, allied health workers, and other relevant stakeholders. Equally, Refs. [28, 29] averred that health care services require multitasking and employing diverse employees with expertise in diversity, public relations, and patient care management, as a formidable team is paramount and teams with diverse personnel and skill mixes can provide high-quality care services and ensure patient safety. A supportive work atmosphere, culture, and structure, strong relationships, problem-solving abilities, good team leadership, task-focused, honest communication, and optimism are essential for these teams to succeed. Furthermore, this diverse set of employees or workforces has different traits that can be aligned with the attributes of Douglas McGregor's Theory X and Y [24, 30]. Theory X (i.e., those people who do not like working but only have an interest in getting remuneration and could only work when forced or threatened with sanctions) and Theory Y (those who like work, see it as part and parcel of their endeavour, and can contribute positively more to the growth of the organisation even if a little motivation is given to them).

Therefore, when leaders, managers, and directors of health facilities are forming a team that will ensure quality health care services to the target audience and the larger society, measures must be put in place to integrate these employees or people with these characters or traits for effective and efficient management of patient care and related service provision. This is because if only a team of Theory Y traits is formed to manage health facilities, in the event of a sudden death or a case of terminal ill health of some cardinal team members, the organisation can be cut short or go to extinction since those with innovative ideas are gone.

On the other hand, when people or employees who possess both traits are engaged, they will learn and share valuable ideas and skill sets in such a way that if one is no longer in the system, her or his absence may not have many negative effects on the organisation and the entire health care service delivery. Due to the high level of hierarchy among medical practitioners in Nigeria, teamwork is severely hindered. In 1985, Decree 10 came into effect, shifting management and administrative skills in Nigerian health care to doctors, who may or may not have significant experience in the area [31].

Health care hierarchies can be detrimental to teamwork as well as to individualised aspects of health care, suboptimal inter- and intra-clinical workflow optimisation, unstable teams, and a lack of inclusion of various health professions. The three main causes of teamwork failure are unclear role definitions, a lack of explicit coordination, and miscommunications. The most significant factors that prevent effective teamwork in health care settings and other organisations include a lack of organisational support, poor communication, a lack of goal orientation, a lack of task prioritisation, a lack of motivation, a lack of delegation, a lack of accountability, a lack of responsibility, a lack of trust, a lack of individual development, a lack of directional unity, a lack of discipline and order, a lack of realistic organisational goals, brain drain, and a high turnover rate.

Equally, the follow serves as hinderance to effective implementation of teamwork in a typical health care facility. Thus:

Communication/Language Barrier: Ref. [32] averred that medical errors and adverse effects are brought on by ineffective teamwork and communication among healthcare professionals and relevant stakeholders. It is worthy of note that, when it comes to resolving the issues pertaining to poor quality service delivery and enhancing patient safety as well as boosting patient satisfaction with healthcare service provision, teamwork is seen as an imperative variable. Also, where team members are well coordinated, improvements in patient care, including quality enhancements and decreases in patient length of stay, are always achieved. Thus, effective teamwork is a pivotal way to solve communication gaps between healthcare providers and patients and among the various health teammates and health partner agencies.

The communication aspect of teamwork is crucial for effective collaboration, proper management of health resources, and decision-making in problem-solving. For a team's work to result in the delivery of high-quality healthcare services in any healthcare facility, communication between teammates, between providers (patients or carers), and other relevant stakeholders is one of the essential components. Communication is the process of transmitting and sharing accurate, reliable, and high-quality data, information, ideas, and knowledge using a suitable language and format that the recipient or teammates can understand, as well as giving feedback to the sender in order to encourage innovation, foster a sense of shared understanding in problem-solving, and gain an advantage over rivals. It is noteworthy that language plays a crucial role in good teamwork and communication. The Babylonians, for instance, built a massive city and tower with its pinnacle in the skies, according to the Holy Bible, in an effort to gain fame.

However, God interfered with the work by making the languages of the expert and non-expert employees, as well as those of the supporting workers, so confusing that they were no longer able to communicate effectively or understand one another well enough to work as a team to accomplish their primary goal. As a result, the city and tower were never finished, and they were scattered across the surface of Earth [32]. In order for a team to properly collaborate and utilise its collective knowledge, good communication is optimal when the appropriate language is used in the exchange of ideas and information between team members. Positive communication contributes to team identification and group cohesion. On the other hand, a lack of communication might cause team members to work too independently and lose sight of how their work affects others. Hence, effective cooperation is made possible by strong communication, which empowers the leader to organise and motivate subordinates to offer high-quality services and dependable goods.

7. Empirical review of teamwork

Arora et al. [30] examined the effectiveness of teamwork in the workplace and found that effective teamwork is crucial for human progress and survival. Results establish that teamwork provides better results for organisations than individual work, but many management personnel still lack the necessary skills to build teams. The study surveyed 225 participants aged 18–80, primarily Hispanic or Latino (56%), white or non-Hispanic (40%), and 4% of other races. Results showed a significant difference between ethnicity and teamwork preference, but no significant difference was found between gender and perceived self-awareness. The findings further indicated that organisations that are open and supportive of cultural diversity in the workplace are more likely to have effective work teams. Some of these findings were supported by the recent findings of Ref. [33], who studied the relationship between team characteristics and job team effectiveness in IT organisations. A survey of 110 information technology professionals revealed that team purpose, goals, roles, processes, and relationships are interdependent. Positive relationships were found between team roles and processes. The study emphasises the importance of investing in various team effectiveness dimensions to develop effective teams. Findings revealed that workplace resilience is crucial for enhancing performance and well-being in challenging circumstances, and other factors like work culture, leadership, and management support are also essential for developing effective teams.

In another development, Ref. [31] conducted an empirical study on perceived organisational support in healthcare, focusing on the importance of teamwork and training for employee wellbeing and patient satisfaction through a serial mediation involving employee well-being and intention to remain. Findings showed that data from both surveys was managed by the Care Quality Commission in partnership with Picker Institute Europe and other regulators of health and social care services in Britain. The findings indicate that teamwork has a positive indirect association with patient satisfaction ($r = 0.43$, $p < 0.01$) through employee well-being (job satisfaction and work engagement) and intention to remain ($r = 0.03$, $p < 0.01$). The strength of this indirect relationship is also enhanced by the training provided by the organisation. The study found that the quality of social relationships and support generated by teamwork activities play a vital role in reducing employees' withdrawal tendencies towards the organisation. Although there was no significant direct relationship between employees' teamwork perceptions and patient satisfaction, the study showed that perceptions of teamwork have a positive indirect influence on patient satisfaction, explained by job satisfaction and intention to remain. These results lend additional support to previous findings by Ref. [34], suggesting that employees' exposure to collaborative team processes is crucial for both employees' and patients' satisfaction.

According to Ref. [34] investigation on health care professional development: working as a team to improve patient care, effective teamwork in health care is crucial for patient safety and outcomes. The need for effective teams is increasing due to co-morbidities and complex specialisations. Findings indicated that the evolution in health care and a global demand for quality patient care necessitate parallel health care professional development with a great focus on patient-centred teamwork. A patient-centred approach is essential for professional development, focusing on values and principles that place the patient at the centre of care. The results further state that motivation and practical skills are essential for team members to achieve goals and overcome challenges, thereby emphasising the importance of teamwork and providing practical approaches to delivering quality patient care.

Consequently, in Iran, Ref. [35] studied the impact of teamwork on an organisation's performance using a cooperative game framework. They compared individual and collective performance indexes and used a cooperative game model to improve organisational performance. The model evaluated employee activities and implemented fair payments, such as overtime pay and rewards, to increase performance and satisfaction. The cooperative approach created effective communication between employees and authorities, enhancing motivation for teamwork. The results could be used for employee decisions, training requirement analysis, employee development, research, and plan valuation. The cooperative coefficient is a key factor in increasing productivity and organisational efficiency. The study found that the cooperative approach directly positively affects teamwork and organisational performance, increasing motivation and satisfaction among employees. These findings connote that when there is effective teamwork among diverse employees in any organisation, seemingly high-quality health care output and patient safety are guaranteed.

8. Summary

Teamwork is crucial for human progress and survival in the workplace. However, many management personnel lack the necessary skills to build teams. It has been established that teamwork has a positive indirect association with patient satisfaction through employee well-being and intention to remain. More so, a cooperative approach directly positively affects teamwork and organisational performance, increasing motivation and satisfaction among employees. Through effective teamwork among diverse employees, seemingly high-quality health care output and patient safety are guaranteed. Importance of teamwork in patient safety, as well-functioning teams commit fewer mistakes, and with high patient acuity, a collaborative approach is crucial for both patients and health care providers' safety. Effective teamwork development has a strong positive correlation with the quality of health care service provision. This suggests that organisational success depends on understanding roles and interdependence within teams.

Teamwork is a vital part of clinical work and patient care but is poorly understood in certain instances. More so, team satisfaction, trust, and strong coordination are crucial for success in the workplace. Despite the importance of teamwork in a health care setting, there are many factors hindering teamwork effectiveness, including the working environment, leadership, government policies, employees' attitudes, and peer support, which significantly impact employee engagement. In a nutshell, an effective team not only protects patients from risks but also creates a more positive, engaging, and resilient workplace. Similarly, effective teamwork leads to positive patient outcomes but is hindered by factors such as doctors' dominance, allied professionals' attitudes, salary disparity, poor communication, and a defective leadership style. Teamwork suffers when healthcare providers are unable to communicate effectively.

9. Suggestion

The provision of health care services is a multifaceted, multitasking activity that calls for a broad workforce, including unskilled, semi-skilled, and skilled workers. As a result, cooperation is essential to patient-centered care and a counterbalance to the provision of high-quality healthcare services. For effective teamwork to be adopted for quality patient care achievement and related issue addressing, the following suggestions are provided, viz.

i. Adequate manpower and other resources should be employed in health care settings.

ii. Leadership should be restructured to align with the organisation's goals and objectives.

iii. Building trust and providing an enabling environment and policies

iv. All stakeholders must be responsible and accountable.

v. There should be training and retraining of team members.

vi. There should be policies that do not hinder individual contributions or stakes in decision-making.

vii. There should be monitoring and evaluation of the delivery of health care services and mechanisms of feedback.

DOI: http://dx.doi.org/10.5772/intechopen.1004541

Conflict of interest

There is no conflict of interest in this study.

Author details

Ikpoko-ore-ebirien Dike Isaruk[1,2]

1 School of Health Information Management Rivers State College of Health Science and Management Technology, Port Harcourt, Nigeria

2 Department of Information Resources Management, Babcock University Ilishan-Remo, Ogun State, Nigeria

*Address all correspondence to: dykeman1974@gmail.com; isaruk0122@pg.babcock.edu.ng

References

[1] Nelson T. The Holy Bible: Genesis Chapter 1:26-28. King James Version. Apapa, Lagos: Hilson Publishers & Distributors Ltd; 3 Oct 2017. Available from: www.hilsonpublishers.com

[2] Nelson T. The Holy Bible: Ecclesiastes Chapter 4:9-12. King James Version. Apapa, Lagos: Hilson Publishers & Distributors Ltd; 3 Oct 2017. Available from: www.hilsonpublishers.com

[3] Nelson T. The Holy Bible: Psalms Chapter 133:1. King James Version. Apapa, Lagos: Hilson Publishers & Distributors Ltd; 3 Oct 2017. Available from: www.hilsonpublishers.com

[4] Nelson T. The Holy Bible: Proverbs Chapter 27:17. King James Version. Apapa, Lagos: Hilson Publishers & Distributors Ltd; 3 Oct 2017. Available from: www.hilsonpublishers.com

[5] Nelson T. The Holy Bible: 1 Corinthians 1:10. King James Version. Apapa, Lagos: Hilson Publishers & Distributors Ltd; 2017. Available from: www.hilsonpublishers.com

[6] Nelson T. The Holy Bible: Hebrew 10:24-25. King James Version. Apapa, Lagos: Hilson Publishers & Distributors Ltd; 3 Oct 2017. Available from: www. hilsonpublishers.com

[7] Sheingold BH, Hahn JA. The history of quality healthcare: The first 100 years 1860-1960. International Journal of African Nursing Sciences. 2014;**1**:18-22. DOI: 10.1016/j.ijans.2014.05.002

[8] Manser T. Teamwork and patient safety in dynamic domains of healthcare: A review of the literature. Acta Anaesthesiologica Scandinavica. 2009;**53**(2):143-151

[9] Mohammed E, McDonald WG, Ezike AC. Teamwork in health care services delivery in Nigeria: A mixed methods assessment of perceptions and lived experiences of pharmacists in a tertiary hospital. Integrated Pharmacy Research and Practice. 2022;**11**:33-45. DOI: 10.2147/IPRP.S331041

[10] Hornby AS. Oxford Advanced Learner's Dictionary of Current English. In: Wehmeier S, Ashby M, editors. 6th ed. New York: Oxford University Press; 2000

[11] LaFasto F, Larson C. When Teams Work Best: 6000 Team Members and Leaders Tell What it Takes to Succeed. Thousand Oaks, CA: Sage; 2001

[12] Mayo AT, Woolley AW. Teamwork in health care: Maximizing collective intelligence via inclusive collaboration and open communication. State of the art and science. AMA. The Journal of Ethics. 2016;**18**(9):933-940. Available from: www.amajournalofethics.org

[13] O'Leary KJ, Johnson JK, Manojlovich M, Goldstein JD, Lee J, Williams MV. Redesigning systems to improve teamwork and quality for hospitalized patients (RESET): Study protocol evaluating the effect of mentored implementation to redesign clinical microsystems. Health Services Research. 2020;**19**(293):1-11. DOI: 10.1186/s12913-019-4116-z

[14] Mousavi E, Kavi E, Larti N, Dorcheh SJ, Gharahzadeh A. The relationship between attitude toward the effectiveness of teamwork and observing safety standards in Isfahan educational hospitals. Revista Latinoamericana de Hipertensión. 2018;**13**(3):271-276. Available from: www. revhipertension.com

[15] Leonard MW, Frankel AS. Role of effective teamwork and communication in delivering safe, high-quality care. Mount Sinai Journal of Medicine. 2011;**78**:820-826

[16] Mughal MU. The impact of leadership, teamwork and employee engagement on employee performances. Saudi Journal Business and Management Studies. 2020;**5**(3):233-244

[17] Warri D. Effects of leadership styles on quality of health services. Journal of Health Sciences and Development. 2022;**5**(1):08-16. Available from: www.innovationinfo.org

[18] Griffin RW, Singh JB. Management Canadian Edition. New Jersey: Houghton Mifflin Company; 1999

[19] Rosen MA, DiazGranados D, Dietz AS, Benishek LE, Weaver SJ. Teamwork in healthcare: Key discoveries enabling safer, high-quality care. American Psychological Association. 2018;**73**(4):433-450. DOI: 10.1037/amp0000298

[20] Uchejeso OM, Etukudoh NS, Chongs ME, Ime DM. Challenges of Inter-Professional Teamwork in Nigerian Healthcare. London, UK: IntechOpen; 2021. pp. 1-15. DOI: 10.5772/intechopen.95414

[21] Ibara EC. Perspectives in Educational Administration. Port Harcourt: Harey Publication Coy; 2010

[22] Sanyal S, Hisam MW. The impact of teamwork on work performance of employees: A study of faculty members in Dhofar university entrepreneurship in the Middle East. IOSR Journal of Business Management. 2018;**20**(3):15-22

[23] Babiker A, El Husseini ME, Al Nemri A, Al Frayh A, Al Juryyan N, Faki MO, et al. Health care professional development: Working as a team to improve patient care. Sudan Journal of Paediatrics. 2014;**14**(2):9-16. Available from: http://www.sudanjp.org

[24] Touma J. Theories X and Y in combination for effective change during economic crisis. Journal of Human Resource and Sustainability Studies. 2021;**9**:20-29

[25] Enabulele O, Enabulele JE. A look at the two-way referral system: Experience and perception of its handling by medical consultants/specialists among private medical practitioners in Nigeria. International Journal of Family & Community Medicine. 2018;**2**(3):86-92

[26] Zajac S, Woods A, Tannenbaum S, Salas E, Holladay CL. Overcoming challenges to teamwork in healthcare: A team effectiveness framework and evidence-based guidance. Frontier in Communication. 2021;**6**:1-20

[27] Stanford FC. The importance of diversity and inclusion in the healthcare workforce. Journal of National Medical Association. 2020;**112**(3):247-249

[28] Pittman P, Chen C, Erikson C, Salsberg E, Luo Q, Vichare A, et al. Health workforce for health equity. Medical Care. 2021;**59**(10 Suppl. 5): S405-S408. Available from: www.lww-medicalcare.com

[29] Koopmans L, Damen N, Wagner C. Does diverse staff and skill mix of teams' impact quality of care in long-term elderly health care? An exploratory case study. BMC Health Services Research. 2018;**18**(988):1-12. DOI: 10.1186/s12913-018-3812-4

[30] Khawam AM, DiDona T, Hernández BS. Effectiveness of teamwork in the workplace. International

Journal of Sciences: Basic and Applied Research. 2017;**32**(3):267-286. Available from: http://gssrr.org/index.php?journal=JournalOfBasicAndApplied

[31] Ogbonnaya C, Tillman CJ, Gonzalez K. Perceived organizational support in health care: The importance of teamwork and training for employee wellbeing and patient satisfaction. Group & Organization Management. 2018;**43**(3):475-503. Available from: http://sro.sussex.ac.uk/id/eprint/78315/

[32] Nelson T. Holy Bible (Genesis 11:1-9), King James Version. Apapa, Lagos: Hilson Publishers & Distributors Ltd; 3 Oct 2017. Available from: www.hilsonpublishers.com

[33] Arora R, Gajendragadkar S, Neelam N. Team effectiveness: A key to success in 'IT organizations. AABFJ. 2023;**17**(1):97-110

[34] Noviyanti MK. The influence of leadership style and teamwork on satisfaction work employee with environment work as moderating variables at public health center X Batam city. Morfai Journal Multidiciplinary Output Research for Actual and International. 2022;**2**(3):553-564. Available from: https://radjapublika.com/index.php/MORFAI

[35] Askari G, Asghri N, Gordji ME, Asgari H, Filipe JA, Azar A. The impact of teamwork on an organization's performance: A cooperative game's approach. Mathematics. 1804;**2020**(8): 1-15. Available from: www.mdpi.com/journal/mathematics

Chapter 3

Multidisciplinary Teamwork and Interprofessional Partnerships in Healthcare Setting: The Critical Ingredients

Walid El Ansari, Kareem El-Ansari, Habiba Arafa and Abdulla Al-Ansari

Abstract

This chapter provides an overview of the components of successful teamworking and partnership working. It outlines the numerous benefits of effective teamwork and its promise for safe, efficient, and quality care for patients. The chapter describes the challenges to effective teamworking in health care, and delineates the stages involved in joint working efforts as they evolve, highlighting the need for specific teamwork enablers at each stage. The chapter then details selected teamwork enablers, namely communication; the requisite expertise and competencies required; leadership and its types that lend themselves to partnership and teamworking; and power issues within multidisciplinary care settings, and their influences on collaboration. The chapter also communicates other critical factors for successful joint working, including personnel factors, personnel barriers, organisational factors, organisational barriers, and power-related factors, highlighting the interplay of many interlacing factors in joint working. Finally, it illustrates important considerations when evaluating joint and teamworking efforts that require attention, whilst emphasizing some challenges frequently encountered when appraising such initiatives, in terms of process, outcome, and impact measures. The chapter concludes by bringing together these factors in a simple model as a useful take home message for practitioners, professionals, and administrators embarking on teamworking and partnership endeavours.

Keywords: teamwork, partnerships, collaboration, interprofessional, multidisciplinary

1. Introduction

Teamworking, partnerships, collaboration, cooperation, coordination, and interorganizational, interagency, or interprofessional working have all been used to describe the broad phenomenon of harmoniously working together in order to deliver outcomes that are usually beyond the reach of any single individual or organization alone. Collaboration and teamwork are commonly interchangeably used terms [1]. Teamwork represents interactions between members of the team who pool their combined resources to complete the required tasks [2]. Any team is a group but not very group is necessarily a team [3]; groups grow into teams when they acquire mutual commitment and synergism among the membership [4].

Patient care is increasingly dependent on the collaboration of healthcare teams of different professional backgrounds, for instance, physicians, nurses, and therapists, to provide quality and comprehensive care. Multi/interdisciplinary teams are standard practice in numerous aspects of the provision of healthcare [5], rendering teamworking critical as such provision is premised on the conduct and attainment of the team rather than that of the individual [6, 7]. Such sharing of labor among physicians, nurses, and allied health practitioners entails that no individual practitioner can dispense a complete experience of care [8]. Increasingly, the maintenance and enhancement of the health of the public in an economically viable manner necessitates team-based care [9, 10]. This is due to the multifold benefits of effective teamworking.

2. Benefits of effective teamwork

Research evidence supports a positive association linking teamworking and care outcomes [11]. Policymakers, practitioners, and academics alike have increasingly underscored teamwork to accomplish safe and patient-centered outcomes, incorporating care across institutional borders, professional groups, and organizational boundaries [12]. An evolving raft of evidence depicts the important significance of teamwork at various stages of the care process and is acknowledged to be a key feature in improving patient care [2, 13]. Given that most care is now delivered by teams of experts and specialists [14], teamwork is characterized as a significant element of health service reform, crucial for care that is safe and efficient [15].

Multidisciplinary teamworking for care that is coordinated has great promise to improve the outcomes of patients while decreasing the costs and is essential for healthcare professionals to enhance efficiency at the same time as to avoid unnecessary harm to the patient [9, 16]. The advantages of efficacious teamworking in healthcare comprise decreased medical mistakes, improved care quality for patients, higher satisfaction of patients, enhanced contentment and retaining of staff, and decreased burnout of the healthcare personnel [17, 18]. Teams who are involved in teamwork procedures and practices are 2.8 times more likely to attain high accomplishment than those who are not [19].

Recently, a systematic review and meta-analysis has observed that care establishments need to acknowledge the benefits and merit of teamworking and highlight strategies and policies that sustain and enhance teamworking for the advantage of their patients [19]. Today, professionals concur that effective teamwork is associated with care that is both safe and effective at many strata of the healthcare organization [20–22]. Moreover, effective teamwork improves control over the working ecosystem and hence results in efficient use of time, effectiveness, satisfied patients, and reduced patient and practitioner strain and worry [23–26].

However, merely establishing a team structure does not necessarily guarantee that it is likely to function effectively [27]. Enhanced and more economically viable patient outcomes are accomplished when health practitioners practice and acquire skills together, audit their clinical outcomes jointly, and transform routines to progress and innovate practice and service delivery [28]. Despite the prospective advantages of teamwork, not everyone wishes to work in teams, because not all teams are effective [6]. Benefits are harvested when better functioning teams make decisions that are of better quality, manage complicated tasks more effectively, and better coordinate activities and expertise [29, 30]. Indeed, the challenges to successful and efficacious teamworking are numerous.

3. Challenges to effective teamwork

It is acknowledged that teamworking in the field of healthcare is complex. Members of the team with different professional backgrounds, education, preparation, understanding, skills, approaches, and outlooks may work in different areas and shifts [31]. The team members' turnover is traditionally high, and members frequently are unfamiliar with each other and might not value the abilities and skills of the individuals they are working with [31]. Furthermore, the power hierarchies that might operate within and between professions could hamper novice staff, or whole practitioner clusters, from being incorporated effectively as full members of the team [7].

Certainly, in practice, interprofessional teamworking could be challenging to accomplish due to a range of causes. These include cultural and training disparities and distinctions between the different professions, seeming and real interprofessional hierarchical pyramids, attitudes of staff and their experiences of working in an interprofessional manner, and the sometimes temporary makeup and sporadic character of teams in care settings [7, 32–34]. Thus, despite the growing evidence on the paybacks and advantages of teamworking care in clinical settings, the healthcare environment might remain rather resilient to the wider application of such team-based care models. This is due to system-wide barriers in addition to difficulties at the level of individual agencies that deliver the healthcare [9].

Enhancing our grasp and knowledge of the ways interprofessional teamworking is navigated and implemented across care and clinical settings is hence critical to guide tailored quality improvement strategies design effective training programs premised on consideration and awareness of the limitations of clinical practice [35].

4. Stages of joint working efforts

It is critical that practitioners and members of any team are conversant with the stage of development of a joint working initiative [36]. The *formation* stage happens at the instigation of funding and establishment of committees. This then progresses to the *implementation* phase, as committees undertake needs assessment to explore and ascertain the concerns of populations they are dealing with and accordingly design and generate intervention policies and strategies. The *maintenance* stage includes the follow-up, scrutiny, and continuation of the committees and actions. Finally, while the *outcome* phase consists of the impacts that were foreseen for the given intervention/s, the implication is that each stage, with its unique tasks, would require unique focus on some of the factors or teamwork enablers more than others (**Figure 1**).

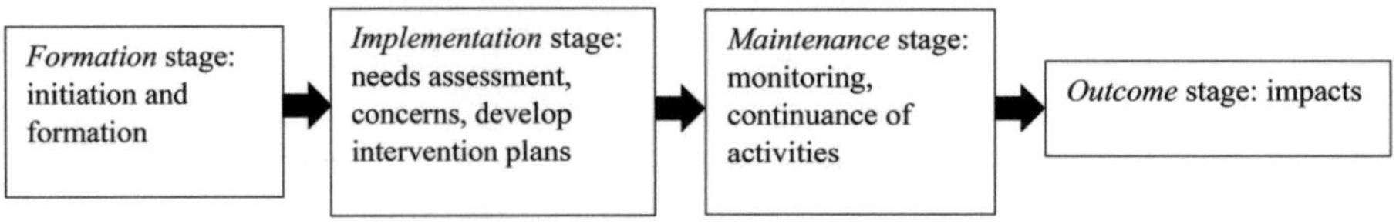

Figure 1.
Stages of development of joint working (adopted from [36]).

5. Teamwork enablers

Successes emanate from the successful implementation of teams, rather than merely having such teams in place. The formation and continuation of operational and successful teams require time and determination and usually necessitate investment [27]. Indeed, members of "pseudo teams" reported observing more errors, incidents, and near misses; underwent more annoyance, bullying, and mistreatment from both the staff and patients; and reported less well-being and more worry and tension than individuals working in real teams [37].

5.1 Communication

Communication is imperative among the entire membership of a clinical team [38]. Increased extents of the tightly linked communication and teamwork are vital to moderate stress and waiting times and enhance patient safety [24], and poor communication and organizational factors were the most common features impeding effective teamwork [6].

Communication among health care professionals (HCP) is influenced by human factors and interpersonal relations [39], where collegial relationships support effective teamwork that results in better outcomes for both the clients and providers (e.g., [40]). However, contrary to teams in other work environments, members of care teams do not automatically view themselves as equals, categorizing themselves in a hierarchical order of HCP that disadvantages both communication and joint working [41]. Such hierarchical differences, power, and conflicts contribute to shaping how communication is instituted in the context of healthcare, causing different professional groups to work in parallel, to the disadvantage of teamworking [42, 43]. Organizational silence and the difficulties some HCP might encounter in expressing themselves in the presence of their coworkers are an obstacle to communication and teamwork [44].

When individuals fail to articulate and voice their worries, the challenges and difficulties that they note remain unchanged, and the culture of silence is further boosted, rendering team members less dedicated and devoted [43]. Malfunctions and disappointments commonly happen when communication is overdue to be helpful; content is neither always complete nor precise; important members are excluded, and concerns remain unsettled until the point of necessity and stress [45]. Most conflict situations occur when one/more member of the team is not appropriately kept in the loop [16]. Collaboration can uncover diverging interests, and joint working can be spoilt and muddled by communication challenges [16]. Communication is a vital competency that is characteristic of many substantially successful teams that operate in many environments and across various disciplines [46]. For instance, for a highly effective endoscopy unit team, efficacious communication is critical between members of the team to avoid unproductive, unhelpful, or even damaging types of communication [47]. For instance, a pertinent example of successful communication for an endoscopy team is that of closed-loop communication which entails a three-step process to ensure effective and clear communication [48].

5.2 Skills, expertise, and competencies

The power of teamworking lies in the collaboration forged between different individuals who possess different skill sets and knowledge, in order to face and solve a joint and collective challenge. Hence, for teams to function successfully and effectively, all members must recognize and appreciate the abilities and capabilities of every individual and coworker in the team [49]. Effective interdisciplinary teams are characterized by having an appropriate and complementary skill and practitioner mix, sufficient competencies, and balance of personalities, together with the capacity to make the most of other team members' experience and timely replacement or cover for empty or absent posts [50].

A systematic literature review on teams within the context of medical care categorized these capabilities into three groups, namely, knowledge (e.g., shared task models, understanding of the situation, acquaintance with team members' characteristics, appreciation of the objectives of the team, and the particular duties attached to each undertaking), skills (e.g., monitoring, adaptability, behavior, leadership of the effort, resolving disagreements and differences, feedback, communication), and attitude (e.g., team alignment and focus, combined effectiveness, collective and mutual vision, team interconnection, mutual trust, value and significance of working in teams) skills [51].

Research has noted that effective healthcare teams require competencies that include familiarity with the organizational objectives, plans, and approaches and dedication of their agencies; mutual respect for other team members; and obligation to joint working in order to attain good value and superior results [52]. Similarly, others highlighted a range of capacity domains that are critical when jointly working in partnership. These included educational capabilities, partnership building and maintenance abilities, engagement skills, change expertise, talents in formulating strategy and managing groups, and that those working in such initiatives need to appreciate and value one other's expertise and abilities [53].

For these reasons, it is critical to select the appropriate team composition [54]. For instance, across endoscopy teams, instigating successful teams required focus on the highly effective qualities and warranted the proper attention to the team's configuration to distinguish the amount of members and responsibilities required to undertake the necessary tasks in order to ascertain that initiatives were run with the appropriate number and quality of individuals needed to be fruitful and productive [47]. If composition appraisal is poor, resulting in a team that has less than optimal number of partners or insufficient participants that have the required competencies, such an effort is not likely to accomplish and achieve [47]. HCP are expected to regularly and consistently have a good flow of information and synchronize and join forces with others both in and beyond their official team, frequently with colleagues from distinctive professions, specializations or teams. Hence, the ongoing processes of "teaming" are the norm, and some authors view that as practically every individual participating in providing healthcare need and hence have teamworking abilities, competencies, and experience above and on top of their clinical expertise [55].

5.3 Leadership

Understanding the influence of leadership as well as systematically appraising its relationships with the accomplishment of outcomes in partnership initiatives and team working is important [56]. Leadership comprises a vital part in teams that operate in difficult settings [57], and within partnership working efforts, the attributes of the leadership, as well as knowledge, dedication, competencies, communication, and interpersonal interactions, are vital in accomplishing the teams' goals [58]. For instance, there is evidence to show that in joint working environments, more than 25% of the leaders' skills were explained by their communication skills and their operational understanding, highlighting the value of these critical qualities for the leaders of collaborative efforts [59]. Indeed, effective leaders are linked to team success, sense of fulfillment, and achievements [60], and in settings where patients were also part of the collaborative effort, respondents who perceived their leadership positively expressed more favorable rankings among 30 other partnership features compared to those who viewed the leadership in a less positive light [61].

A particular type of leadership that resonates with teamworking is shared leadership, described as a sharing and allocation of leadership working relationships, in a way that every member has a distinctive function that is strongly placed in the setting of the group [62]. Healthcare teams face many of the challenges that propel them toward such shared leadership. These include the high complexity of the tasks, as well as a high level of interdependence in settings that are time-sensitive and changing. Generally, leadership of care teams is associated with high workloads [63]; hence, the sharing of leadership responsibilities, duties, and chores may contribute to diminish the cognitive load encountered by leaders [64]. Research indicates that shared leadership might offer a beneficial way forward to enhance the impacts of teams operating in acute care environments [65], and the successes of shared leadership have been recognized in settings characterized by tasks that have great complexity [57].

Certainly, several systematic reviews and meta-analyses across many and varied team and organizational environments have confirmed the positive interactions between shared leadership and team outcomes [66–68]. Shared leadership is recognized to increase the success of team efforts, as well as efficiency and fulfillment and gratification, leading to greater collaboration, coordination, unity, trust and agreement, which collectively decrease the probability of interpersonal disagreements, task tensions, and process clashes [69–71]. Notwithstanding, hierarchical norms that are firmly entrenched in healthcare may offer considerable impediment to the success of shared leadership [72].

Other leadership formats that have been noted to be useful in partnership and teamworking situations include the notion of functional leadership [73]. This notion suggests that successful leaders take on particular leadership activities (e.g., managing personnel/material resources) as necessitated by the team and that leadership is achieved by formally and informally selected leaders. Other types include collaborative leadership that builds upon the concept of involving members in collective problem-solving [74] and content-oriented leadership that focuses on appreciating the duty and on challenges, where such leaders facilitate and encourage the managing of information, presenting the foundation for sense-making to members of the team by information search and exchange [73]. In addition, structuring leadership encompasses channeling and configuring team processes through coordinating the actions of the team such as the allocation of roles and resource management [73].

5.4 Power in multidisciplinary healthcare team settings

Power is the capacity to achieve decisions, act autonomously, and possess control/ influence over others [75]. Fundamental to the concept of collaborative working is the construct of shared power [76]. The inherent features of medical teams might generate many differences in opinions and are associated with thorny issues of the distribution of power within a team [75]. As in generally the case with teams in many contexts, teamworking in medical teams is affected by power differentials and conflict [77, 78].

Historically, healthcare settings have been hierarchical in nature, assigning status to individuals premised on their profession, discipline, and scope of practice [79]. A substantial feature in malfunctions in healthcare settings is unequal power interactions that occur between/among members of the team in an occupational hierarchical pyramid [39, 80]. Power is a function of inter-individual relationships, rather than an attribute of a person [81]. In interdisciplinary settings, teamwork can be impeded by such hierarchy as those team members with less authority are less comfortable sharing their skills and knowledge with others [79]. The key impacts that stem from power discrepancies and disparities include negative influences on team collaboration, decision-making, communication, and overall performance [82, 83]. Researchers have advocated that patient safety research needs to explore and appraise the complicated relationships between power and teamworking in healthcare settings [82].

What emerges is that conflict is inevitable in teamworking [84]. Conflict is a feeling by the parties involved of differences, discrepancies, and mismatched wishes [85]. It can be categorized as task-related conflicts, pertaining to the execution of tasks; relationship conflict, connected to the personality clashes that surface as a consequence of contradictions relating to personal matters; and process conflict that is related to logistical or delegational issues [86, 87]. Such conflict situations might be initiated or perpetuated by differences in the opinions of the members of the team, as there is evidence that different team members or "stakeholders" might perceive the outcomes of their joint working effort differently [88]. Collectively, these situations draw attention to the critical value of interpersonal skills within the team, as well as conflict resolution abilities, and talents in being able to critique and comment on team performance in nonthreatening ways [89]. Successful teamwork is premised on the interlacing connections of various work processes, exchanges of members, and shared and reciprocal recognitions of knowledge and objectives [90]. Hence, team members need to possess and nurture positive and constructive relationships that are critical [91] and to contribute to mediating and resolving any emerging conflicts [25].

5.5 Other factors

A variety of requisite foundations for successful teamworking in healthcare settings have been acknowledged, including organizational and structural support [92, 93]. Teams functioning in primary healthcare are also greatly affected by the funding and organizational provisions of the given health system [94]. An organizational structure is required that facilitates collaboration among players from diverse sectors and specialties [95], as the structure presents and offers a setting for planning, communicating, managing, and evaluating [96]. Good teamwork is a cultivation of these factors.

6. The interplay of factors in joint working efforts

Figure 2 depicts a comprehensive picture of the operational, technical, and conceptual interlacing dimensions that interplay in partnership and teamworking. These comprise personnel factors, for example, expertise: experience; personnel barriers, for example, priorities, availability, and interest; organizational factors, for example, interactions, decision-making, and flow of information; organizational barriers, for example, differences, lack of participation, and goal setting; power-related factors, for example, power disparities, tensions, and team dynamics; as well as other factors, for example, personal traits, motivation, negotiating skills, tolerance, and patience. Attention is required to the barriers that need to be considered by teams. These encompass barriers of organization, of attitude, of vision, and of ignorance [98, 99].

7. Evaluation of joint and teamworking efforts

The wide range of factors that interplay in joint working efforts suggests that evaluations of such initiatives are not going to be straightforward. Evidence on the bearing and outcomes of collaborative efforts is affected by the multiplicity of perspectives and viewpoints of the involved members and conceptual features, as well as challenges in the measurement of the many notions that are included [100]. Some of the factors to be considered include the choice of macro or micro evaluation, of proximal or distal indicators, of short- and long-term effects, or of individual-level or collective-level outcomes. Such assortment in turn suggests the need for mixed methods evaluations using quantitative and qualitative methodologies that capture both the process as well as the outcomes [101]. Whereas measuring the outcomes of team and partnership efforts is necessary to gauge effectiveness, it is usually not sufficient, as in cases where the outcomes are suboptimal; it is only the processes that might be able to explain and shed light on the deficiencies that are encountered. Hence, the variables involved in the process of joint working need to be measured;

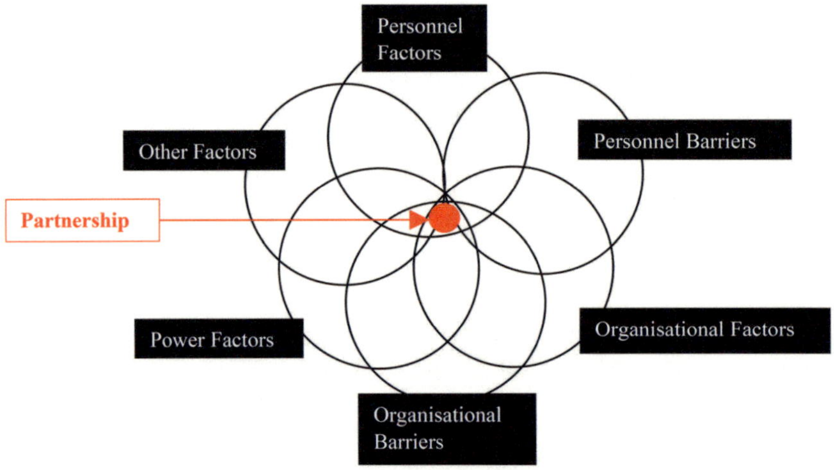

Figure 2.
The multiple dimensions of joint working. Adapted and modified from Rogers et al. [97], Gottlieb et al. [96], El Ansari & Phillips [76].

the analysis of collaborative teamworking as a "process" then becomes imperative. In summary, members value information on whether the team was effective or otherwise (outcomes) and why (process).

8. Conclusion

Due to the numerous features and aspects that blend together to generate an effective collaborative teamworking effort, this chapter outlined insights to the interlacing features necessary for understanding such initiatives. If such efforts are to move past the rhetoric, numerous skills and varied expertise, beyond and above the clinical knowledge and know-how, need to be cultivated in the many facets of these endeavors. For such initiatives to deliver impact, many critical ingredients are requisite for success. In many instances, practitioners, professionals, and administrators might not be fully aware of the raft of intricately interlacing aspects that intertwine to render such schemes effective.

Author details

Walid El Ansari[1,2,3*], Kareem El-Ansari[4], Habiba Arafa[5] and Abdulla Al-Ansari[1]

1 Department of Surgery, Hamad Medical Corporation, Doha, Qatar

2 Clinical Public Health Medicine, College of Medicine, Qatar University, Doha, Qatar

3 Clinical Population Health Sciences, Weill Cornell Medicine-Qatar, Doha, Qatar

4 Faculty of Medicine, St. George's University, Saint George's, Grenada

5 Faculty of Science, Western University, Ontario, Canada

*Address all correspondence to: welansari9@gmail.com

References

[1] Xyrichis A, Ream E. Teamwork: A concept analysis. Journal of Advanced Nursing. 2008;**61**:232-241

[2] Fernandez R, Kozlowski SJ, Shapiro MJ, et al. Toward a definition of teamwork in emergency medicine. Academic Emergency Medicine. 2008;**15**:1104-1112

[3] Arthur H, Wall D, Halligan A. Team resource management: A programme for troubled teams. Clinical Governance: An International Journal. 2003;**8**:86-91

[4] Katzenbach JR, Smith DK. The discipline of teams. Harvard Business Review. 1993;**71**:111-120

[5] Ellingson LL. Communication, collaboration, and teamwork among health care professionals. Communication Research Trends. 2002;**21**(3):1-21

[6] Gafa M, Fenech A, Scerri C, et al. Teamwork in healthcare organisations. Pharmaceutical Education [Internet]. 2018;**5**(2):1-7. Available from: https://pharmacyeducation.fip.org/pharmacyeducation/article/view/151/127 [Accessed: March 20, 2024]

[7] Weller J, Boyd M, Cumin D. Teams, tribes and patient safety: Overcoming barriers to effective teamwork in health care. Postgraduate Medical Journal. 2014;**90**:149-154

[8] Sicotte C, Pineault R, Lambert J. Medical interdependence as a determinant of use of clinical resources. Health Services Research. 1993;**28**:599-609

[9] Landman N, Aannestad LK, Smoldt RK, et al. Teamwork in health care. Nursing Administration Quarterly. 2014;**38**:198-205

[10] New York Academy of Medicine. Interprofessional care coordination: Looking to the future. Policy Research, & Practice. 2013;**1**(2):1-20

[11] Sorbero E, Donna O, Farley DO, et al. Outcome Measures for Effective Teamwork in Inpatient Care. Santa Monica, CA: RAND Corporation; 2008

[12] Dreachslin J, Hunt P, Sprainer E. Workforce diversity: Implications for the effectiveness of health care delivery teams. Social Science & Medicine. 2000;**50**:1403-1414

[13] Valentine MA, Nembhard IM, Edmondson AC. Measuring teamwork in health care settings: A review of survey instruments. Medical Care. 2015;**53**:e16-e30

[14] Kohn LT, Corrigan J, Donaldson MS. To Err Is Human: Building a Safer Health Care System. US: Institute of Medicine, National Academies Press; 2000

[15] Finn R, Learmonth M, Reedy P. Some unintended effects of teamwork in healthcare. Social Science & Medicine. 2010;**70**:1148-1154

[16] Bitter J, van Veen-Berkx E, Gooszen HG, et al. Multidisciplinary teamwork is an important issue to healthcare professionals. Team Performance Management. 2013;**19**:263-278

[17] Clements D, Dault M, Priest A. Effective teamwork in healthcare: Research and reality. Healthcare Papers. 2007;**7**:26-34

[18] Estryn-Behar M, Van der Heijden B, Oginska H, et al. The impact of social work environment, teamwork characteristics, burnout, and personal factors upon intent to leave among european nurses. Medical Care. 2007;**45**:939-950

[19] Schmutz JB, Meier LL, Manser T. How effective is teamwork really? The relationship between teamwork and performance in healthcare teams: A systematic review and meta-analysis. BMJ Open. 2019;**9**:e028280

[20] Salas E, Rosen MA. Building high reliability teams: Progress and some reflections on teamwork training. BMJ Quality and Safety. 2013;**22**:369-373

[21] Schraagen JM, Schouten T, Smit M, et al. A prospective study of paediatric cardiac surgical microsystems: Assessing the relationships between non-routine events, teamwork and patient outcomes. BMJ Quality and Safety. 2011;**20**:599-603

[22] Thomas EJ. Improving teamwork in healthcare: Current approaches and the path forward. BMJ Quality and Safety. 2011;**20**:647-650

[23] Kaissi A, Johnson T, Kirschbaum MS. Measuring teamwork and patient safety attitudes of high-risk areas. Nursing Economy. 2003;**21**:211-218

[24] Kilner E, Sheppard LA. The role of team-work and communication in the emergency department: A systematic review. International Emergency Nursing. 2010;**1**:127-137

[25] Risser DT, Rice MM, Salisbury ML, et al. The potential for improved teamwork to reduce medical errors in the emergency department. Annals of Emergency Medicine. 1999;**34**:373-383

[26] Shapiro MJ, Morey JC, Small SD, et al. Simulation based teamwork training for emergency department staff: Does it improve clinical team performance when added to an existing didactic teamwork curriculum. Quality & Safety in Health Care. 2004;**13**:417-421

[27] Tanco M, Jaca C, Viles E, et al. Healthcare teamwork best practices: Lessons for industry. The TQM Journal. 2011;**23**:598-610

[28] Borrill C, West M, Dawson J, et al. Team working and effectiveness in health care. British Journal of Health Care. 2000;**6**:361-371

[29] Grumbach K, Bodenheimer T. Can health care teams improve primary care practice? Journal of the American Medical Association. 2004;**291**:1246-1251

[30] Wagner EH. The role of patient care teams in chronic disease management. BMJ. 2000;**320**:569-572

[31] Anderson JE, Lavelle M, Reedy G. Understanding adaptive teamwork in health care: Progress and future directions. Journal of Health Services Research & Policy. 2021;**26**:208-214

[32] Chesluk B, Bernabeo E, Reddy S, et al. How hospitalists work to pull healthcare teams together. Journal of Health Organization and Management. 2015;**29**:933-947

[33] Hall P. Interprofessional teamwork: Professional cultures as barriers. Journal of Interprofessional Care. 2005;**19**:188-196

[34] Liberati EG, Gorli M, Scaratti G. Invisible walls within multidisciplinary teams: Disciplinary boundaries and their effects on integrated care. Social Science & Medicine. 2016;**150**:31-39

[35] Lavelle M, Reedy GB, Cross S, et al. An evidence based framework for the

temporal observational analysis of teamwork in healthcare settings. Applied Ergonomics. 2020;**82**:102915

[36] Butterfoss FD, Goodman RM, Wandersman A. Community coalitions for prevention and health promotion. Health Education Research. 1993;**8**:315-330

[37] West MA. Effective Teamwork: Practical Lessons from Organizational Research. 3rd ed. Oxford: Blackwell Publishing; 2012

[38] Rixon S, Braaf S, Williams A, et al. Pharmacists' interprofessional communication about medications in specialty hospital settings. Health Communication. 2015;**30**:1065-1075

[39] Lee CT, Doran DM. The role of interpersonal relations in healthcare team communication and patient safety: A proposed model of interpersonal process in teamwork. The Canadian Journal of Nursing Research. 2017;**49**:75-93

[40] Moore LW, Leahy C, Sublett C, et al. Understanding nurse-to-nurse relationships and their impact on work environments. Medsurg Nursing. 2013;**22**:172-179

[41] Baker L, Egan-Lee E, Martimianakis A, et al. Relationships of power: Implications for interprofessional education. Journal of Interprofessional Care. 2011;**25**:98-104

[42] Bagnasco A, Tubino B, Piccotti E, et al. Identifying and correcting communication failure among health professional working in the emergency department. International Emergency Nursing. 2013;**21**:168-172

[43] Maxfield DG, Lyndon A, Kennedy HP, et al. Confronting safety gaps across labor and delivery teams. American Journal of Obstetrics and Gynecology. 2013;**209**:402-408

[44] da Silva Nogueira JW, Rodrigues MC. Effective communication in teamwork in health a challenge for patient safety. Cogitare Enfermagem. 2015;**20**:630-634

[45] Lingard L, Espin S, Whyte S, et al. Communication failures in the operating room: An observational classification of recurrent types and effects. Quality & Safety in Health Care. 2004;**13**:330-334

[46] McEwan D, Ruissen GR, Eys MA, et al. The effectiveness of teamwork training on teamwork behaviors and team performance: A systematic review and meta-analysis of controlled interventions. PLoS One. 2017;**12**:e0169604

[47] McDonald NM. Learning from highly effective teams: What can we apply to the gastrointestinal endoscopy unit team? ACG Case Reports Journal. 2022;**9**:e00745

[48] Salik I, Ashurst JV. Closed Loop Communication Training in Medical Simulation. Treasure Island, FL: StatPearls Publishing; 2021

[49] Johnson HL, Kimsey D. Patient safety: Break the silence. AORN Journal. 2012;**95**:591-601

[50] Nancarrow SA, Booth A, Ariss S, et al. Ten principles of good interdisciplinary team work. Human Resources for Health. 2013;**11**:19

[51] Baker DP, Salas E, King H, et al. The role of teamwork in the professional education of physicians: Current status and assessment recommendations. Journal of Quality and Patient Safety. 2005;**31**:185-202

[52] Leggat SG. Effective healthcare teams require effective team members:

Defining teamwork competencies. BMC Health Services Research. 2007;7:17

[53] El Ansari W, Phillips CJ, Zwi AB. Narrowing the gap between academic professional wisdom and community lay knowledge: Perceptions from partnerships. Public Health. 2002;**116**:151-159

[54] Shuffler ML, Diazgranados D, Maynard MT, et al. Developing, sustaining, and maximizing team effectiveness: An integrative, dynamic perspective of team development interventions. The Academy of Management Annals. 2018;**12**:688-724

[55] Tannenbaum SI, Greilich PE. The debrief imperative: Building teaming competencies and team effectiveness. BMJ Quality and Safety. 2023;**32**:125-128

[56] El Ansari W. Leadership in community partnerships: South African study and experience. Central European Journal of Public Health. 2012;**20**:174-184

[57] Künzle B, Zala-Mezö E, Wacker J, et al. Leadership in anaesthesia teams: The most effective leadership is shared. Quality & Safety in Health Care. 2010;**19**:e46

[58] Sheaff R, Schofield J, Mannion R, et al. Organisational factors and performance: A review of the literature. In: NHS Service Delivery and Organisation R&D Programme. London, UK: Programme of Research on Organisational Form and Function; 2004. (Reference number: WS15)

[59] El Ansari W, Oskrochi R, Phillips CJ. One size fits all partnerships? What explains community partnership leadership skills? Health Promotion Practice. 2010;**11**:501-514

[60] Kumpfer KL, Turner C, Hopkins R, et al. Leadership and team effectiveness in community coalitions for the prevention of alcohol and other drug abuse. Health Education Research. 1993;**8**:359-374

[61] El Ansari W, Oskrochi R, Phillips C. Engagement and action for health: The contribution of leaders' collaborative skills to partnership success. International Journal of Environmental Research and Public Health. 2009;**6**:361-381

[62] Conger JA, Pearce CL. A landscape of opportunities. Future research on shared leadership. In: Pearce CL, Conger JA, editors. Shared Leadership: Reframing the Hows and Whys of Leadership. Thousand Oaks, CA: SAGE Publications; 2003. pp. 285-303

[63] Tofil NM, Lin Y, Zhong J, et al. Workload of team leaders and team members during a simulated sepsis scenario. Pediatric Critical Care Medicine. 2017;**18**:e423-e427

[64] Janssens S, Simon R, Beckmann M, et al. Shared leadership in healthcare action teams: A systematic review. Journal of Patient Safety. 2021;**17**:c1441-e1451

[65] Aufegger L, Shariq O, Bicknell C, et al. Can shared leadership enhance clinical team management? A systematic review. Leadership in Health Services (Bradford, England). 2019;**32**:309-335

[66] D'Innocenzo L, Mathieu JE, Kukenberger MR. A meta-analysis of different forms of shared leadership–team performance relations. Journal of Management. 2016;**42**:1964-1991

[67] Nicolaides VC, LaPort KA, Chen TR, et al. The shared leadership of teams: A meta-analysis of proximal, distal, and moderating relationships. Leadership Quarterly. 2014;**25**:923-942

[68] Wang D, Waldman DA, Zhang Z. A meta-analysis of shared leadership and team effectiveness. The Journal of Applied Psychology. 2014;**99**:181-198

[69] Bergman JZ, Rentsch JR, Small EE, et al. The shared leadership process in decision-making teams. The Journal of Social Psychology. 2012;**152**:17-42

[70] Wood MS. Determinants of shared leadership in management teams. International Journal of Leadership Studies. 2005;**1**:64-85

[71] Yeatts DE, Hyten C. High-Performing Self-Managed Work Teams: A Comparison of Theory to Practice. Thousand Oaks, CA: Sage Publications; 1998

[72] Currie G, Lockett A. Distributing leadership in health and social care: Concertive, conjoint or collective? International Journal of Management Reviews. 2011;**13**:286-300

[73] Zaccaro SJ, Rittman AL, Marks MA. Team leadership. The Leadership Quarterly. 2001;**12**:451-483

[74] Chrislip DD, Larson CE. Collaborative leadership: How citizens and civic leaders can make a difference. In: American Leadership Forum Book, American Leadership Forum Series. San Francisco: Jossey-Bass; 1994

[75] Janss R, Rispens S, Segers M, et al. What is happening under the surface? Power, conflict and the performance of medical teams. Medical Education. 2012;**46**:838-849

[76] El Ansari W, Phillips CJ. Empowering healthcare workers in Africa: Partnerships in health—Beyond the rhetoric towards a model. Critical Public Health. 2001;**11**:231-252

[77] Booij LHDJ. Conflicts in the operating theatre. Current Opinion in Anesthesiology. 2007;**20**:152-156

[78] Rogers DA, Lingard L. Surgeons managing conflict: A framework for understanding the challenge. Journal of the American College of Surgeons. 2006;**203**:568-574

[79] Krishnakumar D, Caskey R, Hughes AM. Examining the influence of power distance on psychological safety within healthcare teams. In: Proceedings of the International Symposium on Human Factors and Ergonomics in Health Care. Vol. 10(1). Los Angeles, CA: SAGE Publications; 2021. pp. 194-198

[80] Lingard L, Sue-Chue-Lam C, Tait G, Bates J, Shadd J, Schulz V. Pulling Together and Pulling Apart: Influences of Convergence and Divergence on Distributed Healthcare Teams. Advances in Health Sciences Education: Theory and Practice. 2017;**22**(5):1085-1099. DOI: 10.1007/s10459-016-9741-2

[81] Overbeck JR, Park B. Powerful perceivers, powerless objects: Flexibility of powerholders' social attention. Organizational Behavior and Human Decision Processes. 2006;**99**:227-243

[82] Kearns E, Khurshid Z, Anjara S, et al. Power dynamics in healthcare teams–a barrier to team effectiveness and patient safety: A systematic review. BJS Open. 2021;**1**:zrab032-091

[83] Stevens EL, Hulme A, Salmon PM. The impact of power on health care team performance and patient safety: A review of the literature. Ergonomics. 2021;**64**:1072-1090

[84] Jehn KA, Rispens S. Conflict in workgroups. In: Barling J, Shaver P, editors. The Sage Handbook of Organizational Behavior. Vol. 1.

Thousand Oaks, CA: Sage Publications; 2009. pp. 262-276

[85] Boulding KE. Conflict and Defence: A General Theory. New York, NY: Harper & Row; 1963

[86] de Dreu CKW, Weingart LR. Task versus relationship conflict: A meta-analysis. The Journal of Applied Psychology. 2003;**88**:741-749

[87] de Wit FRC, Greer LL, Jehn KA. The paradox of intragroup conflict: A meta-analysis. The Journal of Applied Psychology. 2011;**97**:360-390

[88] El Ansari W. Educational partnerships for public health: Do stakeholders perceive similar outcomes? Journal of Public Health Management and Practice. 2003;**9**:136-156

[89] Despins LA. Patient safety and collaboration of the intensive care unit team. Critical Care Nurse. 2009;**29**:85-91

[90] Gharaveis A, Hamilton DK, Pati D. The impact of environmental design on teamwork and communication in healthcare facilities: A systematic literature review. HERD. 2018;**11**:119-137

[91] Beal DJ, Cohen RR, Burke MJ, McLendon CL. Cohesion and performance in groups: a meta-analytic clarification of construct relations, Journal of Applied Psychology. 2003;**88**(6):989-1004

[92] El Ansari W, Phillips CJ. Interprofessional collaboration: A stakeholder approach to evaluation of voluntary participation in community partnerships. Journal of Interprofessional Care. 2001b;**15**:351-368

[93] Williams G, Laungani P. Analysis of teamwork in an NHS community trust. Journal of Interprofessional Care. 1999;**13**(1):19-28

[94] Pullon S, McKinlay E, Dew K. Primary health care in New Zealand: The impact of organisational factors on teamwork. The British Journal of General Practice. 2009;**59**:191-197

[95] Florin P, Chavis D, Wandersman A, Rich RC. Analysis of dynamic psychological systems: Methods and applications. In: Levine R, Fitzgerald H, editors. Analysis of Dynamic Psychological Systems. New York: Plenum; 1992

[96] Gottlieb NH, Brink SG, Gingiss PL. Correlates of coalition effectiveness: The Smoke Free Class of 2000 Program. Health Education Research. 1993;**8**(3):375-84

[97] Rogers T, Howard-Pitney B, Feighery EC, Altman DG, Endres JM, RoeselerAG.Characteristicsandparticipant perceptions of tobacco control coalitions in California. Health Education Research. 1993;**8**(3):345-57

[98] Allensworth DD, Patton W. Promoting school health through coalition building. Eta Sigma Monograph Series. 1990;7:1-89

[99] Hagebak BR. Getting Local Agencies to Cooperate. Baltimore, MD: University Park Press; 1982

[100] El Ansari W, Phillips CJ, Hammick M. Collaboration and partnerships: Developing the evidence base. Health & Social Care in the Community. 2001;**9**:215-227

[101] El Ansari W, Weiss ES. Quality of research on community partnerships: Developing the evidence base. Health Education Research. 2006;**21**:175-180

Chapter 4

From a Group of People to a Well-Functioning Team: A Transformative Leadership Model in Healthcare

Richard Chivaka

Abstract

This topic deals with the process of transforming a group of people (healthcare workers) into a well-functioning team through a transformative leadership model. One of the biggest challenges in health systems strengthening is that healthcare workers function in silos, as defined by their individual professional disciplines. This compromises service delivery due to poor service integration, duplication of effort, weak referrals, and a toxic work environment. This chapter will focus on the journey that we embark on to implement a transformative leadership model to develop effective and efficient multidisciplinary teams among healthcare workers that in turn drive better and sustainable health outcomes.

Keywords: teams, transformative leadership, healthcare system, trust, change agent, ownership

1. Introduction

In the complex and dynamic landscape of healthcare, the shift from traditional group structures to well-functioning teams has emerged as a pivotal paradigm for achieving optimal patient outcomes, improving operational efficiency, and enhancing the overall quality of healthcare delivery. This chapter delves into the significance of transforming groups into well-functioning teams in healthcare, exploring the multifaceted benefits that effective teamwork brings to this critical sector.

1.1 Importance of teamwork in healthcare

Teamwork in healthcare is fundamental to addressing the intricate and often urgent needs of patients. A substantial body of literature underscores the positive correlation between effective teamwork and improved patient outcomes. Salas et al. [1] and Szalados [2] highlight that cohesive and well-coordinated healthcare teams contribute to reduced medical errors, enhanced patient safety, and increased overall satisfaction among patients. Galleta-Williams et al. [3] investigated the importance of teamwork in preventing burnout and found that teamwork reduced burnout while enhancing staff morale and a sense of accomplishment. Taylor et al. [4], using the COVID-19 lessons, review the psychological principles that underpin healthcare team performance in extreme contexts. Focusing on the concept of resilience as an emergent property of the healthcare system, Khalili et al. [5] argue that team resilience provides a huge opportunity to support team members to effectively manage pressure and deal with stress.

1.2 Transformative leadership: a catalyst for team development

The transformation of healthcare groups into high-performing teams is inherently linked to leadership that transcends traditional models. Van Diggele et al. [6] argue that effective leaders are key in cultivating student leadership qualities during teamwork, which in turn supports the quality of care and improves patient safety. Paganin et al. [7] assert that leadership behavior impacts the culture, direction, and performance of the organization and teams. Transformative leadership, as defined by Bass and Riggio [8], provides a framework for inspiring and motivating individuals to collectively achieve shared goals. In healthcare, transformative leaders play a pivotal role in guiding the evolution of groups into cohesive teams, fostering a culture of collaboration and shared accountability.

1.3 Stages of team development in healthcare

Understanding the stages of team development, as articulated by Tuckman [9]—forming, storming, norming, performing, and adjourning—is crucial in navigating the complexities of healthcare teamwork. Each stage presents unique challenges and opportunities, and transformative leaders guide teams through these phases, ensuring that conflicts are addressed, norms are established, and the team functions cohesively in the pursuit of patient-centric objectives.

1.3.1 Building trust and effective communication

Trust is the bedrock of successful healthcare teams. Peller and Nadler [10] emphasize that patients and team members alike benefit from a foundation of trust. Transformative leaders cultivate trust by fostering open communication channels, encouraging transparency, and creating an environment where individuals feel secure in expressing their opinions and concerns. Sifaki-Pistolla et al.'s [11] research confirmed that trust and performance were closely related and that trust, coupled with years of previous experience, were among some of the key predictors of effective team performance. Effective communication is a linchpin in healthcare teamwork, enabling seamless information flow, quick decision-making, and a more coordinated response to patient needs [12–14].

1.3.2 Empowering healthcare professionals

Transformative leaders empower healthcare professionals by recognizing their expertise, providing autonomy, and creating opportunities for professional growth. Studies, such as those by Laschinger et al. [15, 16], underscore the positive correlation between empowered healthcare professionals and increased job satisfaction, which, in turn, contributes to a more engaged and effective healthcare team. A recent doctoral thesis by Craig [17] revealed that the organization's success depends on transformative leaders' ability to motivate and encourage healthcare teams, transform ideas into achievements, and make decisions that are regarded as unbiased, while communicating effectively with teams.

1.3.3 Diversity and inclusion

In the ever-evolving healthcare landscape, diversity and inclusion are not only ethical imperatives but also contributors to enhanced team performance. Cox [18] emphasizes that diverse teams bring a spectrum of perspectives, ideas, and skills, ultimately leading to improved problem-solving and innovation. Transformative leaders champion diversity and inclusion, creating an environment that values and harnesses differences for the benefit of patient care. Moyinoluwa [14] concludes that transformative leaders enhance team dynamics, staff morale, and patient care by embracing cultural diversity, among other aspects such as effective communication and nurturing emotional intelligence.

1.3.4 Overcoming challenges and measuring success

The transformation of healthcare groups into high-functioning teams is not without its challenges. Transformative leaders, equipped with a deep understanding of these challenges, implement strategies to address them effectively. Metrics and indicators for measuring success in healthcare teams, as highlighted by Mitchell et al. [19], extend beyond clinical outcomes to include patient satisfaction, team cohesion, and adaptability to change. Wespi et al. [20] acknowledge that measuring team performance requires a more holistic approach that entails data triangulation. This involves data from various sources, measuring performance at both individual and team levels, and focusing on both process and outcome measures.

1.4 Conclusion

In conclusion, the significance of transforming groups into well-functioning teams in healthcare is irrefutable. Effective teamwork, guided by transformative leadership, not only improves patient outcomes but also enhances the overall resilience and adaptability of healthcare systems. As the healthcare landscape continues to evolve, the role of transformative leaders in fostering a culture of collaboration, trust, and empowerment becomes increasingly crucial. The ongoing commitment to cultivating well-functioning teams ensures that healthcare remains patient-centric, efficient, and capable of navigating the challenges of the future. The rest of the chapter is organized as follows: Section 2 deals with the importance of teamwork in healthcare, Section 3 discusses challenges encountered in healthcare teamwork, Section 4 presents transformative leadership, while Section 5 discusses the transformative leadership model of excellence in healthcare and how this model of leadership transforms groups of healthcare workers into effective teams. Section 6 deals with the team development journey and the role of transformative leaders at each stage of team development, and Section 7 discusses building trust in healthcare teams and how transformative leadership establishes and maintains trust within these teams. Section 8 discusses ways of overcoming challenges encountered in transforming groups of healthcare workers into teams, while Section 9 deals with ways of evaluating the success of transforming a group of healthcare workers into teams. Section 10 highlights some of the future trends, challenges, and role of transformative leadership in creating well-functioning healthcare teams. Finally, Section 11 provides some recommendations for healthcare leaders looking to implement a transformative leadership model to create well-functioning teams.

2. Importance of teamwork in healthcare

Studies on the role of teamwork in improving outcomes abound. West et al. [21] explored team effectiveness in organizations, including in healthcare, and offered a framework that draws on various theoretical perspectives to comprehensively examine the factors influencing team effectiveness. The study provides insights into various factors that contribute to effective teamwork, such as team composition, leadership, task characteristics, team processes, social identity dynamics, human factors, and ergonomics. The composition of teams, including members' skills, diversity, and interpersonal dynamics, significantly influences team effectiveness. Effective leadership, characterized by clear communication, supportive behavior, and fostering a positive team climate, is crucial for team success. The nature of tasks assigned to the team, including complexity and interdependence, plays a vital role in determining team effectiveness. How teams collaborate, communicate, and make decisions (team processes) is a critical determinant of overall effectiveness. Understanding how individuals perceive their identity within the team and how social dynamics impact cohesion and collaboration is essential. Considering human capabilities and limitations in the design of work systems contributes to effective teamwork.

With specific reference to healthcare, numerous studies have investigated the impact of teamwork on patient outcomes, highlighting the critical role of effective collaboration in healthcare settings. A meta-analysis done by Salas et al. [1] explored the impact of team training on team performance, emphasizing its relevance in healthcare. The study underscored the positive association between team training and improved outcomes. Weaver, Dy, and Rosen [22] investigated the effectiveness of team training interventions in healthcare. The research showed that team training contributes to better communication, coordination, and, ultimately, enhanced patient outcomes. An intensive care unit presents an area in the healthcare system where patient outcomes hold so much weight as families and loved ones are always anxiously waiting for better results. The research done by Reader et al. [23] on interdisciplinary communication in the intensive care unit explored its impact on patient safety. They found out that effective teamwork and communication play a critical role in preventing medical errors and improving patient care. The professional behavior of healthcare workers has a direct bearing on patient outcomes. One key aspect that contributes to the desired professional behavior and, ultimately, better health outcomes is interprofessional collaboration. This is supported by the study done by Zwarenstein and Goldman [24] on interprofessional collaboration, with a focus on the effects of practice-based interventions on professional practice and healthcare outcomes. This study revealed that practice-based interventions that promote interprofessional collaboration positively influence professional behavior and, subsequently, healthcare outcomes. Medical errors can and do cause death, and most of these errors are linked to breakdowns in communication and dysfunctional teamwork. Thus, effective teamwork and collaborative practices have a positive effect on preventing adverse patient outcomes [2, 25].

These studies collectively underscore the importance of teamwork and collaborative practices in healthcare, emphasizing the positive impact on patient safety, quality of care, and overall healthcare outcomes. What is a common strand in all these studies is the role of team collaborative practices in achieving better patient outcomes, as discussed below.

2.1 The role of collaboration in healthcare settings

Collaboration is a cornerstone of effective healthcare delivery, influencing patient outcomes, safety, and the overall quality of care. In today's complex and dynamic healthcare environment, where multidisciplinary teams are commonplace, collaboration plays a pivotal role in addressing diverse patient needs and navigating the intricacies of modern healthcare systems. Here is a closer look at the key aspects of collaboration in healthcare settings:

2.1.1 Patient-centered care

Collaboration among healthcare professionals, including physicians, nurses, therapists, and support staff, ensures the development of individualized treatment plans tailored to the unique needs and preferences of each patient. Collaborative efforts create a holistic approach to patient care, recognizing the interconnectedness of physical, emotional, and social factors impacting health.

2.1.2 Enhanced communication

Collaboration fosters open and effective communication among members of the healthcare team. This interdisciplinary communication is essential for sharing critical information, discussing treatment options, and ensuring seamless transitions in patient care. Also, effective communication within collaborative teams contributes to a reduction in medical errors, enhancing patient safety and minimizing adverse events.

2.1.3 Optimized resource utilization

Collaborative decision-making enables optimal resource utilization. By pooling the expertise of various healthcare professionals, teams can allocate resources efficiently, reducing redundancy and improving cost-effectiveness.

2.1.4 Innovative problem-solving

Team collaboration brings together individuals with diverse skills, knowledge, and perspectives. This diversity fosters innovative problem-solving, allowing teams to explore a range of solutions and approaches to complex healthcare challenges. Collaboration is instrumental in implementing and sustaining quality improvement initiatives. Teams working collaboratively can identify areas for improvement, implement changes, and monitor outcomes effectively.

2.1.5 Transition of care

Collaboration is vital in ensuring the continuity of care, especially during transitions between different healthcare settings (e.g., hospital to home). Effective communication and collaboration at these points prevent gaps in care and improve patient outcomes. Collaborative efforts facilitate seamless care coordination, where various healthcare providers work together to manage and monitor patients with chronic or complex conditions.

2.1.6 Professional development

Collaboration provides valuable learning opportunities for healthcare professionals. Interdisciplinary collaboration allows team members to share knowledge, learn from each other, and stay updated on the latest developments in their respective fields.

2.1.7 Patient engagement

Collaborative healthcare teams involve patients in shared decision-making. This patient engagement fosters a sense of empowerment and ensures that treatment plans align with patients' values and preferences. Collaborative care models often result in improved patient satisfaction, as they perceive a more cohesive and coordinated approach to their healthcare needs.

In conclusion, collaboration is the linchpin of effective healthcare delivery. It not only improves patient outcomes but also enhances the overall efficiency, safety, and quality of care. As healthcare systems continue to evolve, fostering a culture of collaboration remains imperative for addressing the complexities of modern healthcare and ultimately improving the well-being of patients. However, notwithstanding the numerous benefits of healthcare teamwork, it is not without its challenges, as discussed in Section 4.

3. Challenges in healthcare teamwork

Healthcare teamwork is crucial for providing high-quality patient care and achieving positive outcomes. While teamwork in healthcare is seen as not only desirable but imperative, it is also fraught with challenges that test the leadership's resolve to invest in team building. Understanding and addressing these challenges are essential for fostering effective collaboration within healthcare teams. Some common challenges encountered in healthcare teamwork include:

3.1 Communication barriers

Ineffective communication and poor information sharing can lead to misunderstandings, errors, and delays in patient care. This challenge is particularly critical in fast-paced healthcare environments. Also, hierarchical structures in healthcare settings can hinder open communication. Subordinates may be reluctant to voice concerns or suggestions to higher-ranking team members, potentially impacting patient safety.

3.2 Role ambiguity

Ambiguity regarding team members' roles and responsibilities can result in duplication of efforts or important tasks being overlooked. This lack of clarity can contribute to inefficiencies and compromise patient care.

3.3 Limited interprofessional collaboration

In some healthcare settings, professionals from different disciplines may work in silos, limiting interprofessional collaboration. This can impede the comprehensive and holistic care that patients often require. Stereotypes about roles and responsibilities within healthcare teams can hinder collaboration. Overcoming these stereotypes is crucial for fostering a more collaborative environment.

3.4 Time constraints

Healthcare professionals often work in high-stress environments with heavy workloads. Time constraints can limit opportunities for team members to engage in meaningful communication, collaboration, and reflection.

3.5 Resistance to change

Healthcare, by nature, is often slow to adopt changes due to the importance of adhering to proven and standardized practices. This can create resistance to new teamwork methodologies or technologies that could enhance collaboration.

3.6 Cultural and diversity issues

In diverse healthcare teams, cultural variations in communication styles and expectations may lead to misunderstandings. Recognizing and addressing these differences is crucial for effective collaboration. Also, in some situations, language differences among team members and patients can impede effective communication, potentially compromising patient safety and satisfaction.

3.7 Limited training and education

Many healthcare professionals receive limited training in interprofessional collaboration during their education. This lack of preparation may contribute to challenges when they enter the workforce. Regular team-training sessions are essential to enhance collaboration, but resource constraints may limit opportunities for ongoing education and skill development.

3.8 Patient-centered challenges

In some cases, patients may not be adequately involved in the collaborative decision-making process. Including patients in discussions about their care is crucial for achieving patient-centered outcomes.

3.9 Technology integration

While electronic health records (EHRs) offer benefits, challenges in their implementation and use can hinder communication and collaboration among healthcare team members.

Addressing these challenges requires a concerted effort from healthcare organizations, professionals, and policymakers. Implementing strategies such as team training programs, clear communication protocols, and fostering a culture of collaboration can contribute to overcoming these obstacles and improving teamwork in healthcare. Even though transforming groups of healthcare professionals is imperative, it is fraught with difficulties that require strong leadership. The effectiveness of leadership styles in creating well-functioning teams can vary based on factors such as organizational culture, team composition, and the nature of the task at hand. However, according to a meta-analysis by Lowe et al. [26], transformative leadership has been found to be positively associated with teamwork effectiveness. Additionally, a study by Avolio et al. [27] found that transformative leadership behaviors, such as inspirational motivation and individualized consideration, were positively related to team performance. Taylor et al. [4] underscore the key role that leadership plays in developing a well-functioning team. They argue that leaders who foster inclusiveness through openness to new ideas, and being accessible to their team members, help build psychological safety and improve team learning. Section 4 discusses transformative leadership, which transforms a group of healthcare workers into well-functioning teams.

4. Transformative leadership

Transformative leadership is a leadership style that goes beyond traditional models by inspiring and motivating individuals to achieve their full potential and exceed their own expectations. Coined by Burns [28] and later expanded upon by Bass [29], transformative leadership focuses on fostering positive changes in both individuals and organizations. This leadership style aims to create a collective vision, instill a sense of purpose, and empower followers to become leaders themselves [14].

4.1 Key principles of transformative leadership

4.1.1 Inspirational vision

Transformative leaders articulate a compelling and inspirational vision for the future. This vision serves as a guiding force, motivating individuals to transcend their immediate concerns and work toward a shared, meaningful goal.

4.1.2 Intellectual stimulation

Transformative leaders encourage creativity, innovation, and critical thinking among their followers. They stimulate intellectual curiosity, promoting a culture of continuous learning and challenging the status quo.

4.1.3 Individualized consideration

Transformative leaders recognize and value the uniqueness of each individual within the organization. They provide individualized consideration by tailoring their leadership approach to meet the diverse needs and strengths of their followers.

4.1.4 Idealized influence

Leading by example is a fundamental aspect of transformative leadership. Transformative leaders embody the values and behaviors they expect from their followers. They become role models, creating a culture of trust, authenticity, and integrity.

4.1.5 Empowerment

Transformative leaders empower their followers by providing them with autonomy, acknowledging their expertise, and fostering an environment where initiative and creativity are encouraged. This empowerment leads to increased self-efficacy and a sense of ownership among individuals.

4.1.6 Collective vision and mission

Transformative leaders focus on creating a shared vision and mission that align with the values and aspirations of the organization. This collective vision becomes a unifying force that inspires individuals to work collaboratively toward common goals.

4.1.7 Social awareness

Transformative leaders demonstrate social awareness by understanding the needs, concerns, and aspirations of their followers. This awareness enables them to address individual and collective challenges effectively.

4.1.8 Continuous growth and development

Transformative leadership emphasizes continuous growth and development for both the leader and followers. Leaders actively seek opportunities for personal and professional improvement, setting an example for a culture of lifelong learning within the organization.

4.1.9 Ethical and moral leadership

Transformative leaders uphold ethical and moral standards. They make decisions based on principles and values, fostering a culture of integrity, fairness, and ethical conduct within the organization.

In summary, transformative leadership is characterized by its focus on inspiration, empowerment, and positive change. The key principles involve creating an inspirational vision, stimulating intellectual growth, providing individualized consideration, leading by example, empowering followers, and fostering a collective vision that aligns with the organization's values. This leadership style is particularly effective in dynamic and challenging environments where innovation, adaptability, and engagement are crucial for success.

4.2 How transformative leadership goes beyond traditional models

In the dynamic landscape of contemporary organizations, leadership has evolved beyond the conventional models of command and control. Traditional leadership, characterized by top-down decision-making and hierarchical structures, is giving way to a more nuanced transformative leadership approach. Unlike its predecessors, transformative leadership transcends mere oversight and delegation; it inspires and empowers individuals to achieve collective goals while fostering a culture of innovation, collaboration, and continuous growth. Using specific leadership responsibilities and attributes, this section explores how transformative leadership goes beyond traditional paradigms to cultivate a more engaged, cohesive, and resilient healthcare workforce.

4.2.1 Focus on inspiration and vision

Traditional leadership models often prioritize task completion, efficiency, and maintaining the status quo. Transformative leadership goes beyond by emphasizing inspiration and vision. Transformative leaders inspire and motivate individuals with a compelling vision that transcends immediate tasks, fostering a sense of purpose and collective commitment.

4.2.2 Individual empowerment

Hierarchical and directive, traditional leadership often involves top-down decision-making, limiting individual autonomy. Transformative Leadership empowers individuals by providing autonomy and recognizing their unique strengths. Transformative leaders encourage initiative and creativity, fostering a culture of ownership among followers.

4.2.3 Intellectual stimulation

Traditional Leadership typically focuses on maintaining established processes and procedures. Transformative Leadership encourages intellectual stimulation and innovation. Transformative leaders promote critical thinking, curiosity, and a willingness to challenge the status quo, fostering a culture of continuous learning and improvement.

4.2.4 Visionary approach to change

Traditional Leadership is prone to resisting change or implementing it incrementally to minimize disruptions. Transformative Leadership embraces change as an opportunity for growth. Transformative leaders proactively drive positive change, envisioning and implementing transformative shifts within the organization.

4.2.5 Idealized influence

Traditional leadership may lead through authority, rules, and compliance. Transformative Leadership leads through idealized influence. Transformative leaders serve as role models, earning followers' respect and trust through their authenticity, integrity, and adherence to shared values.

4.2.6 Long-term impact

Traditional leadership often focuses on short-term goals and immediate results. Transformative Leadership emphasizes long-term impact. Transformative leaders inspire a commitment to a shared vision that extends beyond immediate tasks, fostering sustainable success and growth.

4.2.7 Relationship building

Traditional Leadership may prioritize task completion over building strong interpersonal relationships. Transformative leadership recognizes the importance of relationships. Transformative leaders actively build positive relationships, creating a supportive environment that enhances collaboration and trust among team members.

4.2.8 Adaptability and flexibility

Traditional Leadership may adhere rigidly to established protocols and routines. Transformative Leadership embraces adaptability and flexibility. Transformative leaders navigate uncertainty and change with resilience, encouraging a culture that thrives on adaptability and continuous improvement.

4.2.9 Inclusive decision-making

Traditional leadership decision-making process is often centralized at the top of the hierarchy. Transformative leadership fosters inclusive decision-making. Transformative leaders engage followers in collaborative decision-making processes, leveraging diverse perspectives and input from the entire team. Traditional leadership primarily focuses on the leader's authority and expertise. Transformative leadership elevates others to leadership. Transformative leaders aim to develop the leadership potential of their followers, creating a culture of shared leadership and collective responsibility.

In essence, transformative leadership transcends the conventional by placing a strong emphasis on inspiration, empowerment, long-term vision, and adaptability. It not only seeks to achieve organizational goals but also strives to elevate individuals and teams to their highest potential, fostering a positive, and impactful organizational culture. The section below delves into how transformative leadership serves as a model for excellence in healthcare.

5. Transformative leadership in healthcare: a model for excellence

The healthcare industry is undergoing a transformative shift, and effective leadership is crucial to navigating this dynamic landscape. As discussed in Section 5, transformative leadership in healthcare is a model that goes beyond traditional leadership approaches, emphasizing inspiration, motivation, and the empowerment of healthcare professionals. This session explores the key principles and components of a transformative leadership model in healthcare and its impact on improving patient outcomes and organizational effectiveness.

Transformative leaders in healthcare articulate a compelling vision that transcends routine tasks. This vision serves as a guiding force, inspiring healthcare professionals to align their efforts with broader organizational goals. Fostering a culture of intellectual stimulation, transformative leaders encourage creativity and innovation among healthcare teams. They recognize the importance of continuous learning and create an environment that supports the exchange of ideas. Transformative leaders recognize the unique strengths and challenges of each healthcare professional. By providing individualized consideration, they tailor their leadership approach to meet the diverse needs of team members, promoting a sense of value and appreciation. Leading by example is a cornerstone of transformative leadership. Healthcare leaders who embody the values and behaviors they expect from their teams create a culture of trust and integrity.

5.1 Components of the transformative leadership model in healthcare

5.1.1 Collaborative decision-making

Transformative leaders in healthcare involve team members in decision-making processes. Collaborative decision-making enhances team cohesion, fosters a sense of ownership, and contributes to innovative problem-solving.

5.1.2 Effective communication

Communication is paramount in healthcare, and transformative leaders prioritize transparent and open communication. They ensure that information flows seamlessly across all levels of the organization, promoting a shared understanding of goals and expectations.

5.1.3 Adaptive leadership

Healthcare is inherently dynamic, and transformative leaders exhibit adaptability. They navigate change effectively, guiding teams through challenges and promoting a culture that embraces continuous improvement.

5.1.4 Empowerment of healthcare professionals

Transformative leaders empower healthcare professionals by providing autonomy, acknowledging their expertise, and fostering an environment where initiative and creativity are encouraged. Empowered professionals are more engaged and committed to delivering high-quality patient care.

5.1.5 Enhanced patient-centric care

A transformative leadership model places a strong emphasis on patient-centric care. Leaders inspire healthcare teams to prioritize the needs and experiences of patients, ultimately leading to improved patient satisfaction and outcomes.

5.1.6 Reduced medical errors

The emphasis on collaboration, open communication, and individualized consideration in transformative leadership contributes to a reduction in medical errors. Team members are more likely to communicate effectively and address potential issues proactively.

5.1.7 Increased staff engagement and satisfaction

Healthcare professionals working under transformative leaders report higher levels of job satisfaction and engagement. Empowered and motivated staff are more likely to provide compassionate and effective care, positively influencing patient experiences.

A transformative leadership model in healthcare is a catalyst for excellence, promoting a culture of innovation, collaboration, and patient-centric care. As the healthcare industry continues to evolve, leaders who embrace the principles of transformation can steer their organizations toward achieving higher levels of effectiveness and improved patient outcomes. Through visionary leadership and a commitment to empowering healthcare professionals, the transformative leadership model stands as a cornerstone for building resilient and successful healthcare organizations.

5.2 Transforming groups into effective teams through transformative leadership

The application of transformative leadership in healthcare settings has been a subject of interest in academic literature, with numerous studies highlighting its relevance and impact on organizational dynamics, employee satisfaction, and patient outcomes. This section explores the literature on the application of transformative leadership in healthcare settings. Prior research has investigated several aspects of transformative leadership in healthcare, such as organizational outcomes, employee motivation, performance and satisfaction [8], impact of transformative leadership on job satisfaction, organizational commitment [30], organizational innovation, creativity and openness to change [31], patient outcomes [32], and work engagement [33].

The seminal work by Bass and Riggio [8] provides foundational insights into transformational leadership. It outlines a causal model linking transformational leadership to organizational outcomes, shedding light on how leaders who inspire and motivate can positively influence employee performance and satisfaction. In the context of the healthcare system, Wong and Cummings [30] study explores the impact of transformational leadership in nursing, emphasizing its positive influence on job satisfaction, organizational commitment, and overall nursing practice. The findings suggest that transformational leadership contributes to creating a supportive and empowering environment for nurses, ultimately enhancing patient care. Cummings et al. [34] research on the impact of leadership on patient outcomes provide evidence that transformative leadership positively impact patience outcomes. The outcome of this research suggests that transformative leadership, characterized by inspirational motivation and intellectual stimulation, positively influences patient care outcomes. Wong and Laschinger's [33] research further provides evidence of how transformative leadership impact positively on healthcare workers' engagement in their work. This study emphasizes the positive impact of transformational leadership on staff nurses. The findings highlight how transformational leaders contribute to creating an engaged and motivated nursing workforce. Cummings et al. [34] study reviewed the various leadership styles in nursing and their impact on the nursing workforce and work environment. In this study, transformational leadership emerges as a significant factor associated with positive outcomes, including job satisfaction and organizational commitment. Cummings et al. [31] examined the link between leadership styles and innovation in nursing organizations. This study suggests that transformative leadership is positively associated with organizational innovation. Hai et al. [35] conclude that the transformative leadership style impacts on organizational performance through an innovative leadership mindset. Transformative leaders foster a culture of creativity and openness to change.

These studies collectively underscore the importance of transformative leadership in healthcare settings, especially in nursing practice. The literature consistently highlights its positive influence on employee engagement, organizational outcomes, and, ultimately, patient care. Transformative leadership, characterized by its emphasis on inspiration, empowerment, and fostering a positive organizational culture, continues to be a valuable area of exploration for improving healthcare leadership practices. Collaborative efforts are paramount in healthcare for delivering high-quality patient care, and transformative leadership holds significant relevance in transforming groups into cohesive and effective teams, as discussed below.

5.2.1 Articulating a compelling vision

Transformative leaders begin by articulating a compelling vision for the future of healthcare delivery. This vision goes beyond routine tasks, inspiring team members with a sense of purpose and a shared goal. A clear and inspiring vision serves as a motivator, aligning the team's efforts toward a collective objective. Team members find motivation in contributing to a meaningful and impactful healthcare mission.

5.2.2 Leading by example

Transformative leaders lead by example, embodying the values and behaviors they expect from their healthcare teams. This authenticity creates a sense of trust and respect among team members. Seeing leaders actively engaged in tasks, demonstrating dedication, and displaying a strong work ethic motivates healthcare teams to emulate these qualities. It fosters a culture of commitment and shared responsibility.

5.2.3 Encouraging intellectual stimulation

Transformative leaders foster intellectual stimulation by encouraging creativity, critical thinking, and innovation within healthcare teams. They create an environment where new ideas are valued and explored. Providing opportunities for intellectual growth and innovation motivates healthcare professionals. The chance to contribute creatively to problem-solving and patient care energizes teams and enhances their sense of professional fulfillment.

5.2.4 Individualized consideration

Transformative leaders recognize the unique strengths and challenges of each team member. They provide individualized consideration by understanding and appreciating the diverse contributions and capabilities within the healthcare team. Feeling acknowledged and valued as individuals inspires team members. Transformative

DOI: http://dx.doi.org/10.5772/intechopen.1005512

leaders leverage this individualized consideration to motivate healthcare professionals to contribute their unique skills and perspectives.

5.2.5 Empowering team members

Transformative leaders empower healthcare professionals by providing autonomy, trusting their expertise, and involving them in decision-making processes. This empowerment fosters a sense of ownership and responsibility. Empowered team members are more motivated to take initiative and actively contribute to patient care. They feel a sense of pride and accomplishment in their work, driving motivation and engagement.

5.2.6 Creating a collaborative environment

Transformative leaders emphasize collaboration, breaking down silos and fostering a sense of unity within healthcare teams. They create an environment where shared goals and mutual support are prioritized. Collaboration inspires motivation as team members feel part of a collective effort. The sense of camaraderie and teamwork motivates healthcare professionals to collaborate effectively, enhancing overall team performance.

5.2.7 Providing support and recognition

Transformative leaders offer support during challenging times, demonstrating empathy and understanding. They recognize the efforts and achievements of healthcare teams, reinforcing a positive and appreciative culture. Feeling supported and acknowledged boosts team morale. Healthcare professionals are motivated when their contributions are recognized, leading to increased job satisfaction and a commitment to achieving shared goals.

5.2.8 Maintaining a patient-centric focus

Transformative leaders instill a patient-centric focus, emphasizing the impact of healthcare teams on patient outcomes. They connect the team's efforts to the well-being of patients, inspiring a sense of purpose and responsibility. Understanding the direct impact on patient lives motivates healthcare professionals. Transformative leaders reinforce the significance of their work in contributing to positive patient outcomes, driving motivation and commitment.

In summary, transformative leaders inspire and motivate healthcare teams by creating a vision that transcends routine tasks, leading by example, fostering intellectual stimulation, providing individualized consideration, empowering team members, promoting collaboration, offering support and recognition, and maintaining a patient-centric focus. These leadership practices contribute to a positive and engaged healthcare workforce dedicated to achieving excellence in patient care. The preceding section has focused on the potential of transformative leadership in transforming a group of healthcare workers into a well-functioning team. However, in both practice and academia, it is acknowledged that team development is not an event but rather a journey that goes through different stages. Therefore, it is important to discuss the attributes of transformative leadership that make this leadership style more pre-disposed to team development throughout the different stages.

6. Team development journey

Understanding the stages of team development is paramount for leaders seeking to nurture effective collaboration and achieve optimal team performance. As teams evolve, they undergo a series of predictable phases, each presenting unique challenges and opportunities. From the initial formation stage marked by uncertainty and individual orientation to the eventual culmination of a cohesive and high-performing unit, navigating these stages requires strategic guidance and adept leadership. This section sets the context for exploring the stages of team development and their implications for fostering teamwork and achieving organizational objectives through transformative leadership.

6.1 Stages of team development

This section, based on Tuckman's [9] stages of group development, is presented as a precursor for discussing how transformative leadership transforms groups of healthcare workers into well-functioning teams. First introduced in 1965, Tuckman's model of group development outlines the various stages that groups typically go through as they form, work together, and accomplish their goals. Tuckman identified four primary stages, later adding a fifth stage in collaboration with Mary Ann Jensen in 1977, as discussed below.

6.1.1 Stage 1: forming

This initial stage is characterized by group members getting to know each other, understanding the group's purpose, and establishing ground rules. Members are often polite and cautious and may seek guidance from the leader. In this stage, the leader plays a crucial role in providing direction and structure during the forming stage, as members are uncertain about their roles and the group's objectives.

6.1.2 Stage 2: storming

In the storming stage, group members start expressing their individual ideas, opinions, and preferences. Conflicts may arise as members assert themselves and vie for positions within the group. This stage is essential for establishing group norms and clarifying expectations. The leader's role involves facilitating open communication, resolving conflicts, and guiding the group through the process of establishing a cohesive identity.

6.1.3 Stage 3: norming

As the group progresses through storming, they begin to resolve conflicts, establish norms, and develop a sense of cohesion. Members start to understand each other better, and a sense of unity emerges. Roles and responsibilities become clearer. In this stage, the leader's role shifts toward facilitating collaboration, reinforcing positive behavior, and supporting the establishment of group norms. Leadership becomes more shared among group members.

6.1.4 Stage 4: performing

In the performing stage, the group operates at its highest level of productivity. Members work together efficiently, utilizing their individual strengths to achieve

DOI: http://dx.doi.org/10.5772/intechopen.1005512

common goals. Communication is open, and the group is capable of independent decision-making. The leader's role in the performing stage is more about delegation and providing support. The emphasis is on maintaining a positive and productive atmosphere while allowing the group to function independently.

6.1.5 Stage 5: adjourning (or mourning)

Added by Tuckman and Jensen [36], this stage acknowledges the temporary nature of many groups. In the adjourning stage, the group concludes its work, and members prepare for disbandment. There might be a sense of accomplishment but also feelings of loss. The leader's role involves acknowledging and addressing emotions related to the group's disbandment. Providing closure, recognizing contributions, and facilitating a positive reflection on the group's achievements are crucial.

It is important to note that while Tuckman's [9] model provides a useful framework, not all groups follow these stages linearly, and some may revisit earlier stages when faced with new challenges or changes. Additionally, the model is not prescriptive but offers insights into the typical dynamics of group development. Further, while the role of the leader has been discussed in a generic way, it is important to focus on how transformative leaders guide teams through these team development stages.

6.2 Role of transformative leadership in team development

6.2.1 Stage 1: forming

Transformative leaders provide a clear and inspiring vision for the team's purpose and goals during the forming stage. This vision helps members understand the collective mission and fosters a sense of purpose. Recognizing the uncertainty in the forming stage, transformative leaders offer support and guidance. They encourage open communication, create a positive atmosphere, and establish initial connections among team members.

6.2.2 Stage 2: storming

Transformative leaders promote open communication during storming, encouraging team members to express their ideas and concerns. This open dialog helps resolve conflicts and ensures that diverse perspectives are considered. Further, transformative leaders actively address conflicts, guiding the team through constructive resolution processes. They emphasize the importance of understanding differing viewpoints and finding common ground to move forward.

6.2.3 Stage 3: norming

Building cohesion is critical in this stage and transformative leaders facilitate the establishment of group norms during the norming stage. They encourage collaboration, emphasizing the strengths of each team member and fostering a culture of mutual support. Recognizing individual strengths, transformative leaders empower team members to contribute their unique skills to the group. This empowerment enhances a sense of belonging and encourages active participation.

6.2.4 Stage 4: performing

In the performing stage, transformative leaders delegate responsibilities and provide team members with autonomy. This allows individuals to utilize their strengths and talents, fostering a sense of ownership and accountability. Transformative leaders support the team's continuous growth by encouraging innovation, celebrating achievements, and promoting a culture of learning. They inspire a commitment to excellence and challenge the team to reach its full potential.

6.2.5 Stage 5: adjourning (or mourning)

Transformative leaders in the adjourning stage acknowledge the team's achievements and contributions. They create opportunities for reflection, emphasizing the positive impact of the team's collective efforts. Recognizing the emotional aspects of adjourning, transformative leaders facilitate closure by addressing feelings of loss and transition. They encourage team members to reflect on their experiences, celebrate successes, and prepare for future endeavors.

Throughout all stages, transformative leaders consistently focus on: (i) continually inspiring team members by reinforcing the overarching vision and emphasizing the meaningful impact of their work, (ii) empowering individuals within the team, recognizing and valuing their contributions, and fostering an environment where everyone feels encouraged to excel, and (iii) adaptability and responsiveness, given the evolving needs and challenges of the team, ensuring that leadership strategies align with the dynamics of each stage. In essence, transformative leaders guide teams through Tuckman's stages by providing vision, promoting open communication, addressing conflicts, fostering collaboration, empowering individuals, encouraging continuous growth, acknowledging achievements, and facilitating closure. This approach contributes to the development of high-performing and resilient teams in dynamic and challenging environments.

While it is evident how transformative leadership builds teams in healthcare following Tuckman's stages, it is important to discuss one central ingredient in the team development process—trust! Without building trust, it is impossible for any leader to turn a group of people into a team. The section below discusses the role of transformative leadership in building trust in healthcare teams. First, the importance of trust in healthcare teamwork is discussed, followed by how transformative leadership builds trust among healthcare teams.

7. Building trust in healthcare teams

7.1 Trust

Trust, in the context of organizational behavior and psychology, can be defined as a psychological state comprising the willingness of an individual or group to be vulnerable to the actions of another party based on the expectation that the other will perform a particular action important to the trustor, irrespective of the ability to monitor or control that other party [37]. Furthermore, Rousseau et al. [38] emphasized the importance of interpersonal trust within organizations, highlighting its role in facilitating cooperation, reducing uncertainty, and enhancing communication among team members. Dirks and Ferrin [39] proposed that trust consists of two key dimensions: (i) cognitive trust, which is based on rational assessments of the trustee's reliability and competence and (ii) affective trust, which involves emotional bonds and feelings of goodwill toward the trustee. Burchard et al. [40] argue that trust in healthcare organizations is bi-directional, as it requires parties involved to assume the role of the trustor while at the same time recognizing their role as trustee. Thus, "trustworthiness" is no longer based solely on healthcare providers' behaviors and credentials but entails the "trustworthiness" and "entrustability" of patients. Therefore, the mutuality and reciprocal nature of trust is critical in understanding not only the role of trust in healthcare teams but in how best to build such trust. These studies contribute to a comprehensive understanding of trust by delineating its cognitive and affective dimensions and underscoring its significance in fostering effective interpersonal relationships and organizational outcomes.

7.2 Role of trust in healthcare teams

The role of trust in healthcare teams is pivotal, influencing communication, collaboration, and overall team effectiveness. Academic research sheds light on the multifaceted nature of trust and its impact on various aspects of healthcare delivery. Several researchers have investigated the process of trust development in healthcare systems, emphasizing the importance of trust among healthcare professionals, administrators, and patients [41–45]. Trust was seen as having a positive impact on collaboration, communication, and the overall functioning of healthcare teams. Pearson et al.'s [46] research agenda paper outlines key areas for studying trust and trustworthiness in healthcare. They explore how trust intersects with various aspects of healthcare, including patient-provider relationships, interprofessional collaboration, and organizational dynamics. Shore et al. [47] investigated the relationship between trust and performance in healthcare teams, focusing on the impact of interpersonal trust among team members. This research showed that trust positively influences team dynamics, communication, and collaboration within healthcare settings. These findings are also supported by Hall et al. [48] study which emphasized that trust is a critical factor in the success of interdisciplinary healthcare teams. In this study, trust among team members was seen as facilitating effective communication, information sharing, and collaboration. However, the study also points out that establishing and maintaining trust is an ongoing process that requires attention to team dynamics, leadership, and open communication strategies. A study exploring trust in teams across various contexts, including healthcare [49], highlighted factors influencing trust, which include (i) perceived team competence, (ii) openness, and (iii) reliability, all of which contribute to a positive team dynamic. This study showed that team trust is associated with improved team performance, effective communication, and knowledge sharing. Calnan and Rowe [50], conducted a critical analysis of trust in healthcare which examined the complex interplay between trust on the one hand, and control and perceived risks, on the other. Trust was identified as a key element in patients' willingness to take risks associated with medical treatments. They concluded that understanding and managing these dynamics is crucial for maintaining a positive patient-provider relationship.

One of the key issues in team building is cooperative behavior within interprofessional healthcare teams. Lee et al.'s [51] study of the association between trust and cooperative behavior in interprofessional healthcare teams provides interesting insights. In this study, trust was found to positively influence collaboration among team members, ultimately impacting patient outcomes. As such, establishing and nurturing trust is vital for fostering a collaborative and patient-centered care approach within teams. Using the ASC-DOC Trust Model Burchard et al. [40] illuminate the dimensions of trust, namely Authenticity, Safety, Consistency, Dependability, Ownership, and Competence. They use the model in the context of physician and patient relationship in which reciprocal exchanges between parties is needed. This model explores trust building in five steps, which entail (i) focusing on the person and their pre-disposition to trusting, (ii) asking for input in a sincere way to understand the person's mind frame, which aids in how to interact with them, (iii) discovering and validating each person's current needs to determine potential trust gaps, (iv) affirming trust that already exist between the parties as baseline for further trust development, and (v) building trust by leveraging the trust baseline to close the trust gaps. Barry et al. [52] argue that there is a need for proper conceptualizations of followership in interprofessional healthcare teams, away from the leader-centric view. Their point is that these teams ought to be seen as composed of active members of interprofessional healthcare teams, where shared leadership models prevail. Barry et al.'s [52] research has implications on how interprofessional healthcare teams are understood, and the role of leadership in developing and sustaining these teams.

These studies collectively contribute to our understanding of trust within the complex dynamics of healthcare teams, shedding light on its implications for team performance, patient outcomes, and the overall functioning of healthcare systems. In summary, trust in healthcare teams is a foundational element that underpins effective collaboration, communication, and patient care. These studies highlight that trust is not only crucial within interdisciplinary teams but also plays a vital role in patient-provider relationships. Fostering and maintaining trust requires attention to interpersonal dynamics, clear communication, and a commitment to reliability and competence, all of which contribute to a positive and efficient healthcare environment. Further, Burchard et al.'s [40] research highlights the importance of developing a way to improve competence and empathy necessary to warrant and gain the trust of patients, and measures that recognize what trust looks and acts like, how to assess its lack, and how to address trust gaps (p. 10). Hall et al. [48] and Taylor et al. [4] point out that establishing and maintaining trust requires, among other things, leadership. Barry et al.'s [52] research supports a different kind of leadership. They argue for the replacement of hierarchy-based team leadership by shared leadership, which is expected to improve team performance within healthcare action teams and emergency situations. The section below explores how transformative leaders establish and maintain trust within teams.

7.3 How transformative leaders establish and maintain trust within healthcare teams

Transformative leaders can establish and maintain trust within healthcare teams by focusing on key levers, such as communication, consistent and reliable actions, creating a shared vision, empowering teams, appreciating and recognizing what is good, resolving conflicts timeously and fairly, team development, and just being human! Below is a discussion of both aspects of establishing and maintaining trust within healthcare teams.

7.3.1 Open and honest communication

Transformative leaders prioritize open and honest communication from the outset. They share information transparently, address concerns proactively, and create an environment where team members feel comfortable expressing themselves. Continuously fostering a culture of open communication, transformative leaders ensure that information flows freely. They actively listen to team members, encourage feedback, and respond authentically to maintain trust. Also, transformative leaders play a crucial role in fostering open and effective communication within healthcare teams by exhibiting several characteristics and practices that contribute to creating a communicative and collaborative environment, such as:

7.3.1.1 Clear vision and goals

Transformative leaders articulate a clear vision and set achievable goals. This clarity provides a common purpose, aligning team members and fostering effective communication toward shared objectives.

7.3.1.2 Active listening

They actively listen to team members, demonstrating empathy and understanding. This encourages open communication, as individuals feel valued and heard, leading to a more transparent exchange of ideas and concerns.

7.3.1.3 Encouraging collaboration

Transformative leaders promote a culture of collaboration where team members feel comfortable sharing their insights and working together. This collaborative environment nurtures open communication channels.

7.3.1.4 Effective feedback

These leaders provide constructive feedback, emphasizing growth and development. By creating a feedback loop, they encourage ongoing communication and improvement, fostering a culture of continuous learning within the team.

7.3.1.5 Empowerment and trust

Transformative leaders empower their team members, trusting them with responsibilities. This trust builds confidence and encourages open communication, as individuals feel empowered to voice their opinions without fear of negative repercussions.

7.3.1.6 Adaptability

They are adaptable and open to change. This flexibility allows for open discussions about improvements and adjustments, fostering a dynamic and communicative environment that adapts to evolving circumstances.

7.3.1.7 Transparent communication

Transformative leaders are transparent about their decisions and the organization's direction. This transparency builds trust and encourages open communication, as team members are more likely to share their thoughts when they understand the context.

7.3.1.8 Leading by example

By modeling effective communication themselves, transformative leaders set the standard for the team. When leaders prioritize open, respectful, and transparent communication, it creates a cultural norm that permeates throughout the organization.

7.3.2 Consistency and reliability

Transformative leaders demonstrate consistency and reliability in their actions. They follow through on commitments, set clear expectations, and uphold a standard of reliability that team members can depend on. Maintaining trust involves a continued commitment to consistency. Transformative leaders deliver on promises, adhere to ethical standards, and model the reliability they expect from their team.

7.3.3 Empowerment and support

Transformative leaders empower team members by trusting them with responsibilities and decision-making. They provide the necessary support, resources, and encouragement to foster a sense of competence and autonomy. Continued empowerment is crucial for maintaining trust. Transformative leaders consistently support and believe in the capabilities of their team members, creating an environment where individuals feel empowered to contribute effectively.

7.3.4 Shared vision and values

Transformative leaders articulate a shared vision and values that resonate with the team. By aligning everyone around a common purpose, transformative leaders create a foundation for trust based on a collective commitment. Consistently reinforcing the shared vision and values is key to trust maintenance. Transformative leaders revisit and emphasize these principles, ensuring that they remain at the forefront of decision-making and actions within the team.

7.3.5 Vulnerability and authenticity

Transformative leaders are willing to show vulnerability and authenticity. By sharing their own challenges and mistakes, they create a culture where openness is celebrated, and team members feel comfortable being authentic. Sustaining trust involves an ongoing commitment to authenticity. Transformative leaders remain genuine, acknowledging their imperfections and fostering an environment where team members feel safe expressing their authentic selves.

7.3.6 Recognition and appreciation

Transformative leaders recognize and appreciate the contributions of each team member. They celebrate achievements, acknowledge hard work, and ensure that individual efforts are valued and acknowledged. Continuous recognition is vital for maintaining trust. Transformative leaders consistently appreciate the efforts of the team, fostering a positive and supportive atmosphere that strengthens the bond among team members.

7.3.7 Conflict resolution

Transformative leaders address conflicts promptly and constructively. They demonstrate a commitment to resolving issues in a fair and equitable manner, ensuring that conflicts are opportunities for growth rather than sources of division. Sustaining trust involves an ongoing commitment to effective conflict resolution. Transformative leaders create a culture where conflicts are approached collaboratively, promoting understanding and resolution.

7.3.8 Investment in development

Transformative leaders invest in the professional and personal development of their team members. This investment demonstrates a commitment to their growth and contributes to building trust through mentorship and guidance. Trust is maintained by continuously supporting the development of team members. Transformative leaders provide opportunities for learning and growth, reinforcing the belief that each team member's success is integral to the overall success of the team.

Transformative leaders establish and maintain trust within teams through open and honest communication, consistency, empowerment, a shared vision, vulnerability, recognition, effective conflict resolution, and a commitment to the development of each team member. By embodying these principles, transformative leaders create a trustful and cohesive team environment that thrives on collaboration and shared success.

In summary, transformative leaders cultivate an environment where open and effective communication is not only encouraged but ingrained in the organizational culture. Through clear vision, active listening, collaboration, empowerment, and transparency, they create a space where team members feel valued and motivated to communicate openly, ultimately contributing to the team's success and growth. While transformative leaders are seen as more effective in transforming groups into well-functioning health teams, the process is not without challenges. The section below discusses how transformative leaders overcome challenges encountered in the process of developing teams.

8. Overcoming challenges in transforming healthcare worker groups into teams

This section focuses on how transformative leaders overcome challenges in transforming groups of healthcare workers into teams. The common challenges in transforming healthcare groups into teams are discussed, followed by how transformative leaders overcome these challenges. Transforming healthcare groups into cohesive and effective teams can be a complex process, and various challenges may impede this transformation. Academic research provides valuable insights into these challenges, shedding light on the factors that hinder the development of high-functioning healthcare teams.

8.1 Common challenges in transforming a group of healthcare workers into teams

The healthcare sector operates within a complex and dynamic environment where effective teamwork is essential for delivering high-quality patient care [12]. However, transforming a group of healthcare workers into a well-functioning team is often fraught with challenges. From navigating hierarchical structures and professional boundaries to addressing communication barriers and fostering interdisciplinary collaboration, healthcare leaders encounter a myriad of obstacles on the path to cohesive teamwork. This section explores the common challenges faced in harnessing the collective potential of healthcare professionals to enhance patient outcomes and organizational performance.

8.1.1 Interprofessional collaboration

Several academic research [52–56] emphasize the challenges associated with fostering collaboration among diverse healthcare professionals. The interdisciplinary nature of healthcare requires effective communication and collaboration, but differing professional backgrounds, roles, and communication styles can pose barriers to seamless teamwork.

8.1.2 Communication barriers

In the paper "Communication and teamworking skills training for health and social care students" [57], the challenges related to communication within healthcare teams are highlighted. Communication breakdowns, including issues with information sharing, unclear roles, and hierarchical communication structures, can hinder the development of effective teams in healthcare settings. Remtulla et al. [58] point to the lack of psychological safety as one key barrier to healthcare team communication. ErJavec et al. [59] extend the understanding of barriers to healthcare team communication by providing additional barriers as differences in communication style between nurse and physician, the lack of a unified structure and language, well-entrenched hierarchical authority structure, and sexism, which complicates nurse-physician communication.

8.1.3 Leadership challenges

Research by Zwarenstein et al. [24] discusses the importance of leadership in interprofessional collaboration. Challenges may arise when there is a lack of strong leadership that can guide the team, set expectations, and foster a collaborative culture. Leadership that does not prioritize teamwork can impede the development of cohesive healthcare teams. Remtulla et al. [58] acknowledge the role played by authoritarian leadership in impeding psychological safety and negatively impacts on

DOI: http://dx.doi.org/10.5772/intechopen.1005512

interprofessional collaboration, even though they argue that team members do have agency in creating psychological safety.

8.1.4 Role ambiguity and conflict

Baggs et al. [60], Kim et al. [61], and Li [62] highlight the presence of role ambiguity and conflicts within healthcare teams. Unclear roles and responsibilities, as well as unresolved conflicts, can hinder team effectiveness. These issues may arise due to differences in professional perspectives, conflicting priorities, or a lack of clarity regarding team objectives. Carbone et al. [63] point out that profound changes in the roles of physicians and nurses in recent years have given rise to overlapping competencies, which in turn create problems related to autonomy and interprofessional collaboration. Ferro et al. [64] focus on the importance of managerial coaching to reduce role ambiguity, further highlighting the need to address the impact of role ambiguity in the ensuing conflict within healthcare teams.

8.1.5 Limited time and resources

In a study on teamwork in healthcare, West et al. [65] discuss challenges related to limited time and resources in healthcare settings. Healthcare professionals often face time constraints and resource limitations, impacting their ability to engage in collaborative activities, training, and other initiatives that promote effective teamwork. Rawlinson et al. [66] concluded that a lack of human resources and time are organizational constraints that negatively affect the implementation of organizational changes, such as team reorganization and coordination.

8.1.6 Resistance to change

Weiner et al. [67] identify resistance to change as a common challenge. Transforming a group into a team often involves changes in roles, workflows, and communication patterns. Resistance to these changes can impede the successful transition to a collaborative team structure. Perceived threats to professional identity, role definition and poor communication represent central challenges for interprofessional collaboration [66].

In conclusion, academic research highlights several challenges in transforming healthcare groups into teams, including interprofessional collaboration issues, communication barriers, leadership challenges, role ambiguity, conflicts, limited time and resources, and resistance to change. Recognizing and addressing these challenges is crucial for fostering effective teamwork in healthcare settings and improving patient outcomes, as discussed below.

8.2 Transformative leaders' strategies to overcome group transformation challenges

Transformative leaders employ various strategies to overcome challenges in transforming healthcare groups into effective teams. Academic research provides insights into these strategies, offering guidance on how transformative leaders can navigate and address the complexities associated with fostering collaborative healthcare teams.

8.2.1 Promoting interprofessional education

The study by Reeves et al. [68] emphasizes the importance of interprofessional education. Transformative leaders can facilitate training programs that expose healthcare professionals to the unique perspectives and roles of different disciplines. This approach helps break down professional silos and promotes a shared understanding among team members.

8.2.2 Enhancing communication skills

Transformative leaders invest in communication skills training for team members, ensuring that they can convey information clearly, listen actively, and navigate diverse communication styles within the team. Several studies underscore the significance of effective communication in interprofessional collaboration [69–71]. Ansa et al. [69] research revealed that interprofessional communication was ranked as the most important Interprofessional Education Collaborative core competence. Advocating for the use of psychology principles to enhance team communication, Grunberg et al. [72] make the case for the use of informal social communication to leverage the power of frequent interactions to increase opinions, attitudes, behaviors, and social cohesion.

8.2.3 Fostering transformational leadership styles

A study by Cummings et al. [32], "Leadership styles and outcome patterns for the nursing workforce and work environment: A systematic review," highlights the positive impact of transformational leadership in healthcare settings. Transformative leaders inspire and motivate team members, creating a collaborative culture. By adopting transformational leadership styles, leaders can address resistance to change, build trust, and promote a shared vision for the team. Farahnak et al. [73] results revealed that transformational leadership influences staff to have positive attitudes toward their work and the use of the evidence-based practice.

8.2.4 Implementing team-training programs

Transformative leaders can implement structured team training initiatives that focus on improving teamwork, communication, and problem-solving skills. In the paper "Team training in healthcare: A narrative synthesis of the literature" [74], the authors discuss the benefits of team training programs. These programs provide opportunities for healthcare professionals to practice collaborative strategies in a controlled environment. Ali et al. [75] research concludes that transformational leadership style of the project manager intensifies project success through team-building, team-building practices and teamwork quality.

8.2.5 Establishing clear roles and responsibilities

Research by D'Amour et al. [76] emphasizes the importance of clarifying roles and responsibilities in collaborative settings. Transformative leaders work toward defining clear roles for each team member, minimizing ambiguity, and establishing a shared understanding of individual contributions. This helps prevent conflicts arising from role ambiguity. Further, the advent of the integration of new technologies in healthcare has ushered in an environment where leaders need to proactively redesign roles, be sensitive to interdependencies, and offer opportunities for collective learning about new technologies, while ensuring that the emerging knowledge of new technologies is distributed across roles [77].

8.2.6 Encouraging continuous learning and adaptability

Continuous learning has been demonstrated as key for teams to remain current and thus able to meet patient needs [78, 79]. By focusing on the potential for flexibility and creativity at the point of care [80], transformative leaders promote a culture of continuous learning and adaptability within healthcare teams [81]. This approach helps teams to foster a positive work environment, stay abreast of industry developments, navigate complexities in the healthcare sector, adopt new technologies, and adapt to evolving patient needs.

8.2.7 Addressing time and resource constraints

Research by Salas et al. [1] addresses challenges related to limited time and resources. Transformative leaders advocate for the allocation of resources to support team-building activities, training programs, and initiatives that enhance teamwork. Olatoye et al. [81] argue that resource constraints necessitate "leadership styles that are creative and innovative, often aligning with adaptive or transformational approaches to navigate challenges effectively" (p. 2027). Prioritizing and optimizing resource utilization is essential for overcoming constraints.

In conclusion, transformative leaders leverage strategies such as promoting interprofessional education, enhancing communication skills, fostering transformational leadership styles, implementing team-training programs, establishing clear roles, encouraging continuous learning, and addressing time and resource constraints to overcome challenges in transforming healthcare groups into effective teams. These strategies contribute to building collaborative and high-performing healthcare teams that positively impact patient care and outcomes. Of course, there is always going to be the question of how to measure success in the process of transforming a group of healthcare workers into a well-functioning team. This is not an easy question to address because most of the changes are not easily quantifiable, let alone the time lag between effort and results. Evaluating the success of team transformation in healthcare involves assessing various metrics and indicators to ensure that the transformation efforts lead to improved patient outcomes, enhanced collaboration, and overall organizational effectiveness. Academic studies provide insights into key metrics and indicators that can be utilized to evaluate the success of team transformation initiatives in healthcare settings. The metrics and indicators used to measure the success of team transformation in healthcare are discussed below.

9. Evaluating the success of transforming a group of healthcare workers into teams

Measuring the success of transforming a group of healthcare workers into a well-function team requires tracking both process and outcome measures.

9.1 Process measures

Process measures refer to the developmental milestones that provide evidence that siloed efforts of group members have given way to coordinated team efforts. They are metrics or indicators used to assess the activities, procedures, or steps involved in carrying out a particular process within an organization. In the context of assessing the success of healthcare team transformation, these measures focus on evaluating the efficiency, effectiveness, and adherence to established protocols or standards exhibited by teams during the execution of tasks or workflows. Below are specific metrics that can be used to assess whether efforts aimed at transforming groups of healthcare workers into teams are working.

9.1.1 Team communication

Team communication can be measured using Communication Effectiveness Scores. This can be done through surveys, feedback and face-to-face observation of how healthcare workers communicate with each other. Shifts and patterns from survey results, augmented by feedback and direct observation about how healthcare workers are communicating with each other, provide useful insights into team cohesion. The study by Kim et al. [82] explored what makes communication effective in healthcare teams. Measuring communication effectiveness through surveys or using tools like communication audits, incident reports, or team assessments provides insights into how well teams are functioning post-transformation. Such metrics help in identifying areas for improvement in communication, crucial for enhancing teamwork. However, self-reporting or observational bias may impact accuracy, and assessing the true impact on outcomes can be challenging.

9.1.2 Staff engagement

Staff engagement is one indicator of how well teams are working. To measure this indicator, Staff Engagement Surveys can be used. Regular surveys assessing staff engagement levels can help gauge the impact of team transformation on the workforce, Cummings et al. [34]. These surveys measure staff satisfaction, motivation, and commitment, indicating the success of team transformation in creating a positive work environment. They reflect the impact of transformation on team dynamics and staff well-being. The downside of this metric is that the survey responses may be influenced by external factors, and survey tools may not capture nuanced feelings or opinions. Morgan et al. [83] research used several measures, such as readiness to collaborate and behavioral trust, process and goal clarity, and role ambiguity to measure team development success.

9.1.3 Reduced turnover rates

While staff turnover can be caused by a myriad of factors, one such cause is a lack of a sense of belonging. Therefore, Staff Turnover Rates can be used to gauge how well groups of healthcare workers have transitioned into well-functioning teams, thus providing each other with a sense of belonging. Lower turnover rates among healthcare professionals indicate increased satisfaction and commitment, which can be linked to successful team transformation, Wong et al. [84]. It is important to bear in mind external factors, such as economic conditions, which may influence turnover rates, causing team transformation effort results to vary.

9.1.4 Workflow efficiency

If teams have properly formed and are functioning well, workflow efficiencies are expected to improve. Thus, time-to-treatment and patient throughput can be used to measure how well work is being properly coordinated in a team environment, where silos are fewer and far between, leading to few cases of things falling through the cracks. A study titled "Impact of communication errors in hospitals" by Cohen et al. [85] underscores the significance of efficient workflows in patient care. Metrics related to time-to-treatment and patient throughput can reflect the impact of team transformation on operational efficiency, which provides tangible measures of process improvements. It is important to note that changes in efficiency metrics may result from various factors, and isolating the effect of team transformation can be complex.

9.1.5 Clinical quality indicators

A lot is said about continuous quality improvement in healthcare systems, and yet not much is said about the relationship between quality compliance/quality improvement and team functioning. Here, Compliance with Clinical Guidelines and Quality Improvement Metrics can be used to measure how well teams are functioning well. Neily et al. [86] study entitled "Association between implementation of a medical team-training program and surgical mortality" highlights the role of team training in improving clinical outcomes. Assessing adherence to clinical guidelines, patient safety metrics, and quality improvement indicators provides a quantitative measure of improved clinical care resulting from team transformation. Please note that changes in clinical quality indicators may result from multiple interventions, making it challenging to attribute improvements solely to team transformation.

9.1.6 Collaborative decision-making

A group of healthcare workers hardly provides an environment within which collaborative decision-making takes place. As such, using shared decision-making scores or team-based decision-making processes as metrics that reflect how well healthcare workers are collaborating in a team environment is important. Murrells et al. [87] explored the impact of teamwork on nursing care. Assessing shared decision-making using shared decision-making scores can provide insights into the success of team transformation in fostering collaborative approaches to patient care. Of course, caution should be practised when using these metrics because subjective measures may vary, and the impact on patient outcomes may be indirect and challenging to quantify.

The above are examples of process measures that can be used to track how well healthcare teams are functioning, and thus point to the effectiveness of the transformative leadership efforts in transforming a group into a well-functioning healthcare team. What is then needed is to look at what happens on the patient care side, as discussed below.

9.2 Outcome measures

Outcome measures refer to metrics or indicators used to evaluate the results, effects, or impacts of an intervention, program, or process. These measures assess the ultimate goals or objectives that an organization seeks to achieve, such as improvements in patient health outcomes, customer satisfaction, financial performance, or other key performance indicators. Outcome measures provide valuable insights into the effectiveness, success, and overall impact of initiatives, allowing organizations to gauge their performance, track progress toward desired outcomes, and make informed decisions for continuous improvement. Outcome measures are at the patient level, since investments in transforming groups into teams are aimed at improving patient health outcomes.

9.2.1 Patient outcomes

Reduction in Adverse Events and Hospital Acquired Infections (HAIs) are good metrics used to measure patient outcomes arising from a well-function team. A study by Landrigan et al. [88] titled "Temporal trends in rates of patient harm resulting from medical care" emphasized the importance of patient safety metrics. Monitoring adverse events and HAIs provides valuable insights into the impact of team transformation on patient outcomes. Other patient outcomes metrics include mortality rates, readmission rates, and complication rates to assess the impact of team transformation on patient outcomes. Such metrics provide concrete measures of the team's effectiveness in delivering quality care and improving patient health. Graupner et al. [89] found that the use of patient-reported outcome measures improved symptom control, health-related quality of life, patient satisfaction and patient-doctor communication. These metrics should be used with caution as they may also be influenced by factors beyond the team's control, making it challenging to attribute changes solely to team transformation efforts.

9.2.2 Patient satisfaction

To measure patient satisfaction, patient satisfaction scores can be used as a metric to provide feedback about how well the healthcare team is working. Glickman et al. [90] discuss the correlation between patient satisfaction and healthcare quality. Evaluating patient satisfaction scores can indicate the success of team transformation efforts in creating a positive patient experience. Surveys and feedback mechanisms gauge patient satisfaction Graupner et al. [89], reflecting the perceived quality of care and interpersonal aspects of the team's performance. Such surveys offer insights into the patient experience and can guide improvements in communication and patient-centered care. However, just like the patient outcomes metrics, these surveys can be subject to biases, and scores may not capture all aspects of the patient's perspective.

In conclusion, evaluating the success of team transformation in healthcare requires a comprehensive approach that considers patient outcomes, satisfaction, team communication, staff engagement, turnover rates, workflow efficiency, clinical quality indicators, and collaborative decision-making. Academic studies provide valuable frameworks and evidence supporting the use of these metrics in assessing the impact of team transformation initiatives on healthcare delivery and organizational performance. While these metrics offer valuable insights into different aspects of team transformation, it is crucial to consider their limitations and the potential influence of external factors. A holistic approach, combining various metrics and qualitative assessments, provides a more comprehensive understanding of the success of team transformation efforts in healthcare.

10. Future trends, challenges and the role of transformative leadership

Emerging trends in healthcare teamwork reflect the evolving landscape of healthcare delivery, emphasizing collaboration, innovation, and patient-centered care. Here are some key trends supported by relevant research findings.

10.1 Interprofessional collaboration

A study by Zwarenstein et al. [24] titled "A systematic review of interprofessional collaboration" emphasizes the importance of interprofessional collaboration in healthcare. Collaborative practices among diverse healthcare professionals contribute to improved patient outcomes and enhanced healthcare delivery. Challenges in fostering effective collaboration among diverse healthcare professionals may arise, impacting the implementation of interprofessional care models. Reeves et al. [68] highlight the role of transformative leadership in promoting interprofessional collaboration. Spaulding et al. [91] point to the need to (i) engage in assessing the long-term impact of interprofessional education, (ii) objectively assess change in collaborative behavior, and (iii) assess the impact of interprofessional education on patient-centered outcomes. Leaders can encourage shared goals, facilitate communication, and address professional silos to enhance collaboration among healthcare team members.

10.2 Digital health and telemedicine collaboration

The integration of digital health tools and telemedicine platforms facilitates collaborative care, allowing healthcare teams to coordinate and communicate effectively, especially in remote or underserved areas [92]. Integrating data-driven decision-making into healthcare teams may face technological and cultural barriers. Leveraging data analytics, transformative leaders can play a crucial role in creating a data-driven culture [93]. In the aftermath of COVID-19, the long-term efforts in this area may entail the development of a National Emergency Tele-Critical Care Network (NETCCN) to ensure an effective response to future emergencies [94]. Transformative leaders can invest in staff training, promote the use of analytics tools, invest in emergency response networks, and ensure that the team is equipped to translate data insights into actionable strategies for continuous improvement.

10.3 Patient-centered care teams

Patient-centered care teams lead to multidisciplinary team of providers and staff working together to cover the full care cycle for a given condition [95]. Within this care model, patients actively participate in decision-making, and research has shown positive effects on health outcomes and resource utilization [96]. Shifting toward patient-centered care teams may face resistance or difficulties in altering traditional care delivery models. Transformative leaders can champion the patient-centered approach, ensuring that the team's vision aligns with delivering personalized, patient-focused care [96]. Transformative leaders can also address cultural shifts and provide support during the transition.

10.4 Team-based learning and training

A study by Eppich and Cheng [97] titled "Health care teams' ability to learn from experiences: A systematic review of health care team training" explores the impact of team training. The research underscores the importance of ongoing team-based learning and training initiatives to enhance communication, collaboration, and overall team effectiveness. Implementing ongoing team-based learning and training initiatives may face challenges related to time constraints or a lack of resources. Eppich and Cheng [97] underscore the importance of team training, and transformative leaders can prioritize and allocate resources for continuous learning. Burgess et al. [98] and Considine et al. [99], asset that team training facilitates deeper engagement and learning, and provides, an opportunity for role modeling of interpro¬fessional collaboration. Transformative leaders can advocate for the development of a supportive learning culture, fostering a commitment to ongoing training initiatives among healthcare professionals.

10.5 Innovative team structures

The research by Roch et al. [100] examines the impact of team structures on patient outcomes. The study suggests that innovative team structures, such as collaborative care models and accountable care organizations, can positively influence patient outcomes. Innovations in healthcare teamwork may need to navigate complex regulatory environments, posing challenges in balancing innovation with compliance. Transformative leaders can navigate regulatory challenges by advocating for policies that support innovation while ensuring compliance with healthcare regulations. Research on leadership and organizational change, such as Cummings et al. [34], emphasizes the importance of leadership in navigating complex healthcare environments.

10.6 Behavioral health integration

Integrating behavioral health into primary care settings enhances collaborative efforts between mental health professionals and primary care teams, addressing both physical and mental health needs [101, 102]. Healthcare professionals may resist changes in team structures, workflows, or the adoption of digital health solutions. Research by Weiner et al. [67] suggests that transformative leaders play a crucial role in overcoming resistance to change. They can communicate a compelling vision, foster a culture of innovation, and involve team members in the decision-making process, promoting a sense of ownership and readiness for change.

These emerging trends in healthcare teamwork align with a broader shift toward patient-centered, collaborative, and technology-enabled care. Continued research and implementation of these trends have the potential to reshape healthcare delivery, improving outcomes and experiences for both patients and healthcare professionals. While transformative leadership can contribute significantly to addressing emerging trends in healthcare teamwork, certain challenges may arise. These emerging trends present potential challenges and opportunities for transformative leadership as they adapt to remain effective in transforming a group of healthcare workers into a well-functioning team. As evidenced by various academic studies, transformative leaders can adapt to challenges associated with emerging trends in healthcare teamwork. Through effective communication, a commitment to innovation, fostering a culture of continuous learning, and addressing resistance to change, transformative leaders can guide health-care teams in successfully navigating the evolving landscape of healthcare delivery.

11. Recommendations for healthcare leaders

For leaders in the healthcare landscape, be they Ministry of Health leaders, development partners (funder and NGOs) and other stakeholders who are looking to implement a transformative leadership model to develop well-functioning teams, here are a few key recommendations.

11.1 Embrace interprofessional collaboration

Foster collaboration among diverse healthcare professionals to enhance patient outcomes. Reeves et al. [68] and Spaulding et al. [91] emphasize the importance of interprofessional collaboration in improving professional practice and healthcare outcomes. Leaders should encourage shared goals, effective communication, and teamwork.

11.2 Address resistance to change

Overcome resistance by communicating a compelling vision, involving team members in decision-making, and fostering a culture of innovation. Weiner et al. [67] highlight the role of transformative leaders in conceptualizing and measuring organizational readiness for change. Leaders can address resistance through effective communication and creating a culture receptive to transformation [73].

11.3 Promote continuous learning and training

Prioritize ongoing team-based learning and training initiatives to enhance communication, collaboration, and overall team effectiveness. Eppich and Cheng's [97] systematic review emphasizes the importance of healthcare teams' ability to learn from experiences. Mlambo et al. [103] argue that access to continuing professional development should be made more attainable, realistic, and relevant, and more resources should be invested in continuous professional development. Leaders should invest in continuous learning initiatives, fostering a culture of adaptability and skill development.

11.4 Leverage data-driven decision-making

Create a data-driven culture by investing in staff training, promoting analytics tools, and translating data insights into actionable strategies. Bates et al. [104] and Adler-Milstein et al. [93], discuss the importance of leveraging data analytics for patient-centered value-added care. Transformative leaders play a crucial role in driving the adoption of data-driven decision-making within healthcare teams.

11.5 Champion patient-centered care

Align the team's vision with delivering personalized, patient-focused care, emphasizing shared decision-making and active patient participation. Rosenthal et al. [96] highlight the impact of patient-centered care teams on health services utilization and costs. Leaders should champion a patient-centered approach, ensuring that the team's values align with delivering individualized care.

11.6 Navigate regulatory challenges with innovation

Cummings et al. [34] stress the importance of leadership in navigating complex healthcare environments. In order to navigate regulatory complexities, it is important to bring an innovative approach while ensuring compliance with healthcare regulations [105]. Transformative leaders can balance innovation with compliance, advocating for policies that support positive changes in healthcare delivery.

11.7 Build a human-centered design approach

Apply human factors and ergonomics principles to healthcare teamwork to improve workflows, reduce errors, and enhance overall team performance. In this regard, Carayon et al. [106] emphasize the significance of human-centered design in home health care. Clarke and Cameron [107] argue that dealing with disrespect and burnout requires human-centered design, where leading with empathy and engaging with authenticity brings about a deeper understanding of problems and the concomitant solutions. Leaders can integrate principles of human factors to enhance the design of healthcare processes and workflows.

11.8 Promote team-based structures

Explore innovative team structures, such as collaborative care models and accountable care organizations, to positively influence patient outcomes [108, 109]. Leaders should consider and implement team structures that promote collaboration and accountability.

Therefore, healthcare leaders looking to implement a transformative leadership model should focus on fostering collaboration, addressing resistance to change, promoting continuous learning, leveraging data-driven decision-making, championing patient-centered care, navigating regulatory challenges, adopting a human-centered design approach, and exploring innovative team structures. These key takeaways provide actionable insights for leaders seeking to navigate the complexities of modern healthcare and drive positive transformation within their teams.

12. Conclusion

The transformative leadership model has a significant impact on healthcare teams, fostering positive changes in team dynamics, collaboration, and overall organizational effectiveness. Transformative leaders inspire and articulate a compelling vision for healthcare teams, aligning members around shared goals and a common purpose. This fosters a sense of direction and collective commitment. They promote a collaborative culture within healthcare teams, breaking down silos and encouraging interdisciplinary communication. This enhances teamwork, leading to improved patient care and outcomes. Transformative leaders effectively manage resistance to change by communicating transparently, involving team members in decision-making, and creating a culture that embraces innovation. This facilitates smoother transitions and acceptance of new practices. The transformative leadership model promotes a culture of continuous learning within healthcare teams. Leaders invest in training and development, ensuring that team members acquire new skills, adapt to evolving challenges, and stay abreast of industry advancements. Leveraging data and analytics to inform decision-making within healthcare teams, transformative leaders promote evidence-based practices, which in turn improve patient care strategies and optimize workflows. As champions of patient-centered care, transformative leaders focus on emphasizing shared decision-making, individualized care, and active patient participation. This shift enhances the overall patient experience and satisfaction. Transformative leaders navigate complex regulatory environments by advocating for policies that support innovation while ensuring compliance. This enables healthcare teams to balance regulatory requirements with a focus on positive changes in care delivery. Through promoting human-centered design, transformative leaders integrate human factors and ergonomics principles into healthcare teamwork, optimizing workflows, reducing errors, and enhancing overall team performance. The transformative leadership model encourages leaders to explore and implement innovative team structures, such as collaborative care models and accountable care organizations. This positively influences patient outcomes and enhances accountability. Finally, by fostering a positive work environment, providing a clear vision, and supporting professional development, transformative leaders contribute to increased job satisfaction and enhanced performance among healthcare team members.

In summary, the transformative leadership model positively impacts healthcare teams by inspiring vision, fostering collaboration, addressing resistance to change, promoting continuous learning, leveraging data-driven decision-making, championing patient-centered care, navigating regulatory challenges, adopting human-centered design, and exploring innovative team structures. These elements collectively contribute to improved team dynamics, patient outcomes, and the overall effectiveness of healthcare delivery.

Author details

Richard Chivaka[1,2]

1 University of Cape Town, Graduate School of Business, Cape Town, South Africa

2 Spark Health Africa, South Africa

*Address all correspondence to: richard@sparkhealthafrica.co.za

References

[1] Salas E, Reyes DL, McDaniel SH. The science of teamwork: Progress, reflections, and the road ahead. American Psychologist. 2018;**73**(4):593-600

[2] Szalados JE. The science of teamwork in healthcare: Importance to patient outcome. In: Szalados JE, editor. The Medical-Legal Aspects of Acute Care Medicine. Cham: Springer; 2021. DOI: 10.1007/978-3-030-68570-6_8

[3] Galleta-Williams H, Esmail A, Grigoroglou C, Zghebi SC, Zhou AY, Hodkinson A, et al. The importance of teamwork climate for preventing burnout in UK general practices. European Journal of Public Health. 2020;**30**(Suppl. 4):iv36-iv38

[4] Taylor AM, Tannenbaum SI, Thomas EJ, Salas E. Helping healthcare teams save lives during COVID-19: Insights and countermeasures from team science. American Psychologist. 2021;**76**(1):1-13. DOI: 10.1037/amp0000750

[5] Khalili H, Lising D, Kolcu G, Thistlethwaite J, Gilbert J, Langlois S, et al. Advancing health care resilience through a systems-based collaborative approach: Lessons learned from COVID-19. Journal of Interprofessional Care. 2021;**35**(6):809-812. DOI: 10.1080/13561820.2021.1981265

[6] Van Diggele C, Roberts C, Lane S. Leadership behaviours in interprofessional student teamwork. BMC Medical Education. 2022;**22**:834. DOI: 10.1186/s12909-022-03923-5

[7] Paganin G, De Angelis M, Pische E, Violante FS, Guglielmi D, Pietrantoni L. The impact of mental health leadership on teamwork in healthcare organizations: A serial mediation study. Sustainability. 2023;**15**:7337. DOI: 10.3390/su15097337

[8] Bass BM, Riggio RE. Transformative Leadership. 2nd ed. New York: Psychology Press; 2006

[9] Tuckman BW. Developmental sequence in small groups. Psychological Bulletin. 1965;**63**(6):384-399

[10] Peller J, Nadler JT. Understanding and improving patient and staff safety with effective teamwork. Joint Commission Journal on Quality and Patient Safety. 2008;**34**(6):335-342. DOI: 10.1016/s1553-7250(08)34042-0

[11] Sifaki-Pistolla D, Melidoniotis E, Dey N, Chatzea VE. How trust affects performance of interprofessional health-care teams. Journal of Interprofessional Care. 2020;**34**(2):218-224. DOI: 10.1080/13561820.2019.1631763

[12] Dartiguelongue JB, Cafiero PJ. Communication in health care teams. Argentine Archives of Pediatrics. 2021;**119**(6):e589-e593

[13] Leonard M, Graham S, Bonacum D. The human factor: The critical importance of effective teamwork and communication in providing safe care. Quality & Safety in Health Care. 2004;**13**(Suppl. 1):i85-i90

[14] Moyinoluwa FL. Transformative leadership strategies in healthcare: A panacea for fostering a positive work environment. British Journal of Multidisciplinary and Advanced Studies. 2024;**5**(2):1-11. DOI: 10.37745/bjmas.2022.0452

[15] Laschinger HKS, Finegan J, Shamian J. The impact of workplace

empowerment, organizational trust on staff nurses' work satisfaction and organizational commitment. Health Care Management Review. 2001a;**26**(3):7-23. DOI: 10.1097/00004010-200107000-00002

[16] Laschinger HKS, Finegan JE, Shamian J, Wilk P. A longitudinal analysis of the impact of workplace empowerment on work satisfaction. Journal of Organizational Behavior. 2001b;**25**(4):527-545

[17] Craig AN. Empowering healthcare workers through transformational leadership [Doctoral dissertations and Projects. 3496]. 2022. Available from: https://digitalcommons.liberty.edu/doctoral/3496

[18] Cox T. Cultural Diversity in Organizations: Theory, Research, & Practice. San Francisco, Calif: Berrett-Koehler; 1994

[19] Mitchell R, Boyle B, Parker V, Giles M, Joyce P. Managing in health care: A systematic review of the evidence for a primary health care perspective. BMC Health Services Research. 2009;**9**(1):248. DOI: 10.1186/1472-6963-9-248

[20] Wespi R, Birrenbach T, Schauber SK, Manser T, Sauter TC, Kämmer JE. Exploring objective measures for assessing team performance in healthcare: An interview study. Frontiers in Psychology. 2023;**14**:1232628. DOI: 10.3389/fpsyg.2023.1232628

[21] West MA, Borrill CS, Dawson JF, Brodbeck F, Shapiro DA, Haward B. Leadership clarity and team innovation in health care. The Leadership Quarterly. 2001;**12**(3):339-364. DOI: 10.1016/s1048-9843(01)00091-1

[22] Weaver SJ, Dy SM, Rosen MA. Team-training in healthcare: A narrative synthesis of the literature. BMJ Quality and Safety. 2014;**23**(5):359-372. DOI: 10.1136/bmjqs-2013-001848

[23] Reader TW, Flin R, Mearns K, Cuthbertson BH. Interdisciplinary communication in the intensive care unit. British Journal of Anaesthesia. 2007;**98**(3):347-352. DOI: 10.1093/bja/ael372

[24] Zwarenstein M, Goldman J, Reeves S. Interprofessional collaboration: Effects of practice-based interventions on professional practice and healthcare outcomes. Cochrane Database of Systematic Reviews. 2009;**3**:1-29, CD000072. DOI: 10.1002/14651858.CD000072.pub2

[25] Zajac S, Woods A, Tannenbaum S, Salas E, Holladay CL. Overcoming challenges to teamwork in healthcare: A team effectiveness framework and evidence-based guidance. Frontiers in Communication. 2021;**6**:606445. DOI: 10.3389/fcomm.2021.606445

[26] Lowe KB, Kroeck KG, Sivasubramaniam N. Effectiveness correlates of transformational and transactional leadership: A meta-analytic review of the MLQ literature. The Leadership Quarterly. 1996;**7**(3):385-425. DOI: 10.1016/s1048-9843(96)90027-2

[27] Avolio BJ, Zhu W, Koh W, Bhatia P. Transformational leadership and organizational commitment: Mediating role of psychological empowerment and moderating role of structural distance. Journal of Organizational Behaviour. 2004;**25**:951-968

[28] Burns JM. Leadership. New York, N.Y: Harper & Row; 1978

[29] Bass BM. Leadership and Performance beyond Expectations. New York, N.Y: A Division of Macmillan Inc.; 1985

[30] Wong CA, Cummings GG. The relationship between nursing leadership and patient outcomes: A systematic review. Journal of Nursing Management. 2010;**18**(6):714-724. DOI: 10.1111/j.1365-2834.2010.01126.x

[31] Cummings GG, MacGregor T, Davey M, Lee H, Wong CA, Lo E, et al. Leadership styles and outcome patterns for the nursing workforce and work environment: A systematic review. International Journal of Nursing Studies. 2010;**47**(3):363-385. DOI: 10.1016/j.ijnurstu.2009.08.006

[32] Cummings GG, Tate K, Lee S, Wong CA, Paananen T, Micaroni SPM, et al. Leadership styles and outcome patterns for the nursing workforce and work environment: A systematic review. International Journal of Nursing Studies. 2018;**85**:19-60

[33] Wong CA, Laschinger HKS. Authentic leadership, performance, and job satisfaction: The mediating role of empowerment. Journal of Advanced Nursing. 2013;**69**(4):947-959. DOI: 10.1111/j.1365-2648.2012.06089.x

[34] Cummings GG, Hayduk L, Estabrooks CA, Mitton CR, Norton PG. The contribution of hospital nursing leadership styles to 30-day patient mortality. Nursing Research. 2008;**57**(5):312-321

[35] Hai TN, Van TT, Thi HN. Relationship between transformational leadership style and leadership thinking of provincial administration leaders. Emerging Science Journal. 2021;**5**(5). DOI: 10.28991/esj-2021-01307

[36] Tuckman BW, Jensen MAC. Stages of small-group development revisited. Group & Organization Management. 1977;**2**(4):419-427. DOI: 10.1177/105960117700200404

[37] Mayer RC, Davis JH, Schoorman FD. An integrative model of organizational trust. Academy of Management Review. 1995;**20**(3):709-734

[38] Rousseau DM, Sitkin SB, Burt RS, Camerer C. Not so different after all: A cross-discipline view of trust. Academy of Management Review. 1998;**23**(3):393-404

[39] Dirks KT, Ferrin DL. Trust in leadership: Meta-analytic findings and implications for research and practice. Journal of Applied Psychology. 2002;**87**(4):611-628

[40] Burchard MA, Grunberg N, Barry ES. Toward Understanding and Building Trust for Practicing and Emerging Healthcare Professionals: The ASC-DOC Trust Model [version 1] MedEdPublish 2020. 2020;9:280. DOI: 10.15694/mep.2020.000280.1

[41] Anderson LA, Dedrick RF. Development of the Trust in Physician scale: A measure to assess interpersonal trust in patient-physician relationships. Psychological Reports. 1990;**67**(3):1091-1100

[42] Dugan E, Trachtenberg F, Hall MA, Culpepper L. Development of abbreviated measures to assess patient trust in a physician, a health insurer, and the medical profession. BMC Health Services Research. 2005;**5**(1):64

[43] Safran DG, Taira DA, Rogers WH, Kosinski M, Ware JE Jr, Tarlov AR. Linking primary care performance to outcomes of care. Journal of Family Practice. 1998;**47**(3):213-220

[44] Thom DH, Ribisl KM, Stewart AL, Luke DA, Further JA. Further validation and reliability testing of the Trust in Physician Scale. Medical Care. 1999;**37**(5):510-517

[45] Hall MA, Fabian C, Elizabeth D, Rajesh B. Trust in the Medical Profession: Conceptual and Measurement Issues. Health Services Research. 2002;**37**(5):1419-1439. DOI: 10.1111/1475-6773.01070

[46] Pearson SD, Raeke LH, Lipsitz SR. Reducing patient harm: A focus on designing safer systems. Health Affairs. 2000;**19**(5):80-90

[47] Shore LM, Randel AE, Chung BG, Dean MA, Holcombe Ehrhart K, Singh G. Inclusion and diversity in work groups: A review and model for future research. Journal of Management. 2011;**37**(4):1262-1289. DOI: 10.1177/0149206310385943

[48] Hall P, Weaver L, Grassau PA. Theories, relationships and interprofessionalism: Learning to weave. Journal of Interprofessional Care. 2015;**29**(3):221-227. DOI: 10.3109/13561820.2014.980937

[49] De Jong JD, Heiligers PJ, Groenewegen PP, Hingstman L. Why are some medical specialists working part-time, while others work full-time? Health Policy. 2016;**120**(2):129-136. DOI: 10.1016/j.healthpol.2015.11.007

[50] Calnan M, Rowe R. Researching trust relations in health care: Conceptual and methodological challenges—An introduction. Journal of Health Organization and Management. 2006;**20**(5):349-358. DOI: 10.1108/14777260610701818

[51] Lee TH, McGlynn EA, Safran DG. A framework for increasing trust between patients and the organisations that care for them. JAMA. 2019;**321**(6):539-540. DOI: 10.1001/jama.2018.19186

[52] Barry ES, Teunissen P, Varpio L. Followership in interprofessional healthcare teams: A state-of-the-art narrative review. BMJ Leader. 11 Sep 2023;**0**:1-7. DOI: 10.1136/leader-2023-000773

[53] Brandt BF, Lutfiyya MN. Making interprofessional education work: The strategic roles of the academy. Academic Medicine. 2012;**87**(11):1-5. DOI: 10.1097/ACM.0b013e318263fe68

[54] Reeves S, Hean S. Why we need theory to help us better understand the nature of interprofessional education, practice and care. Journal of Interprofessional Care. 2013;**27**(1):1-3. DOI: 10.3109/13561820.2012.698328

[55] Reeves S, Perrier L, Goldman J, Freeth D, Zwarenstein M. Interprofessional education: Effects on professional practice and healthcare outcomes (update). Cochrane Database of Systematic Reviews. 2013;**2013**(3):CD002213. DOI: 10.1002/14651858.CD002213.pub3

[56] Thistlethwaite JE, Forman D, Matthews LR, Rogers GD, Steketee C, Yassine T. Competencies and frameworks in interprofessional education: A comparative analysis. Academic Medicine. 2014;**89**(6):869-875. DOI: 10.1097/ACM.0000000000000234

[57] Curtis JR, Treece PD, Nielsen EL, Gold J, Ciechanowski PS, Shannon SE, et al. Randomized trial of communication facilitators to reduce family distress and intensity of end-of-life care. American Journal of Respiratory and Critical Care Medicine. 2013;**188**(2):241-249. DOI: 10.1164/rccm.201208-1430OC

[58] Remtulla R, Hagana A, Houbby N, Ruparell K, Aojula N, Menon A, et al. Exploring the barriers and facilitators of psychological safety in primary care teams: A qualitative study. BMC

Health Services Research. 2021;**21**:269. DOI: 10.1186/s12913-021-06232-7

[59] Erjavec K, Knavs N, Bedenčič K. Communication in interprofessional health care teams. Journal of Health Sciences. 2022;**12**(1):29-37

[60] Baggs JG, Schmitt MH, Mushlin AI, Mitchell PH. Association between nurse-physician collaboration and patient outcomes in three intensive care units. Critical Care Medicine. 1999;**27**(9):1991-1998. DOI: 10.1097/00003246-199909000-00039

[61] Kim Y, Cho HH, Choi E. Effects of nursing work environment and job conflict on turnover intention in hospital nurses. Journal of Korean Academy of Nursing Administration. 2016;**22**(4):375-384. DOI: 10.11111/jkana.2016.22.4.375

[62] Li D. On role conflict and role ambiguity: The case of social workers in healthcare teams. International Healthcare Review. 2022. DOI: 10.56226/40

[63] Carbone R, Ferrari S, Belperio S, Bravi S, Mancinelli C, Soave E, et al. Advanced competence in intensive care unit: Expectations, role ambiguity between physicians and nurses in intensive care units. Multi-method survey. Acta Biomed. 2021, 2021;**92**(Suppl. 2):e2021332. DOI: 10.23750/abm.v92iS2.12670

[64] Ferro AL, Swiger PA, Yoder LH. The relationship between managerial coaching and role ambiguity among nurses in the military health system. Nursing Outlook. 2024;**72**(3):102149. DOI: 10.1016/j.outlook.2024.102149

[65] West MA, Armit K, Loewenthal L, Eckert R, West T, Lee A. Leadership and Leadership Development in Healthcare: The Evidence Base. The Faculty of Medical Leadership and Management; 2014. Available from: https://assets.kingsfund.org.uk/f/256914/x/6577e5c839/leadership_in_health_care_report_february_2015.pdf

[66] Rawlinson C, Carron T, Cohidon C, Arditi C, Hong QN, Pluye P, et al. An overview of reviews on interprofessional collaboration in primary care: Barriers and facilitators. International Journal of Integrated Care. 2021;**21**(2):32. DOI: 10.5334/ijic.5589

[67] Weiner BJ, Amick H, Lee S-YD. Review: Conceptualization and measurement of organizational readiness for change: A review of the literature in health services research and other fields. Medical Care Research and Review. 2008;**65**(4):379-436

[68] Reeves S, Pelone F, Harrison R, Goldman J, Zwarenstein M. Interprofessional collaboration to improve professional practice and healthcare outcomes. Cochrane Database of Systematic Reviews. 2016;**2016**(6):CD000072

[69] Ansa BE, Zechariah S, Gates AM, Johnson SW, Heboyan V, Leo GD. Attitudes and behaviour towards interprofessional collaboration among healthcare professionals in a large academic medical centre. Healthcare. 2020;**8**(3):323. DOI: 10.3390/healthcare8030323

[70] Buring SM, Bhushan A, Broeseker A, Conway S, Duncan-Hewitt W, Hansen L, et al. Interprofessional education: Definitions, student competencies, and guidelines for implementation. American Journal of Pharmaceutical Education. 2009;**73**(4):59. DOI: 10.5688/aj730459

[71] Lee KR, Kim EJ. Relationship between interprofessional communication and team task

performance. Clinical Simulation in Nursing. 2020;**43**:44-50. DOI: 10.1016/j.ecns.2020.02.002

[72] Grunberg NE, McManigle JE, Barry ES. Applying classic social psychology principles to improve healthcare teams. MedEdPublish. 2021;**9**:251, pp.1-14. DOI: 10.15694/mep.2020.000251.2

[73] Farahnak LR, Ehrhart MG, Torres EM, Aarons GA. The influence of transformational leadership and leader attitudes on subordinate attitudes and implementation success. Journal of Leadership and Organizational Studies. 2020;**27**(1):98-111. DOI: 10.1177/1548051818824529

[74] Hughes AM, Gregory ME, Joseph DL, Sonesh SC, Marlow SL, Lacerenza CN, et al. Saving lives: A meta-analysis of team training in healthcare. Journal of Applied Psychology. 2016;**101**(9):1266-1304. DOI: 10.1037/apl0000122

[75] Ali H, Chuanmin S, Ahmed M, Mahmood A, Khayyam M, Tikhomirova A. Transformational leadership and project success: Serial mediation of team-building and teamwork. Frontiers in Psychology. 2021, 2021;**12**:689311. DOI: 10.3389/fpsyg.2021.689311

[76] D'Amour D, Ferrada-Videla M, San Martin Rodriguez L, Beaulieu MD. The conceptual basis for interprofessional collaboration: Core concepts and theoretical frameworks. Journal of Interprofessional Care. 2005;**19**(Suppl. 1):116-131. DOI: 10.1080/13561820500082529

[77] Agreli H, Huising R, Peduzzi M. Role reconfiguration: What ethnographic studies tell us about the implications of technological change for work and collaboration in healthcare. British Medical Journal Leader. 2021;**5**(2):134-141. DOI: 10.1136/leader-2020-000224

[78] Baker DP, Day R, Salas E. Teamwork as an essential component of high-reliability organizations. Health Services Research. 2006;**41**(4 Pt 2):1576-1598. DOI: 10.1111/j.1475-6773.2006.00566.x

[79] Salas E, Cannon-Bowers JA, Johnston JH. The impact of cross-training on team functioning: An empirical investigation. Human Factors. 1997;**39**(4):429-436. DOI: 10.1518/001872097778543886

[80] Younger SJ. Leveraging advanced practice nursing in complex health care systems. Nursing Administration Quarterly. 2020;**44**(2):127-135

[81] Olatoye FO, Elufioye OA, Okoye CC, Nwankwo EE, Oladapo JO. Leadership styles and their impact on healthcare management effectiveness: A review. International Journal of Science and Research Archive. 2024;**11**(01):2022-2032. DOI: 10.30574/ijsra.2024.11.1.0271

[82] Kim LY, Giannitrapani KF, Huynh AK, Ganz DA, Hamilton AB, Yano EM, et al. What makes team communication effective: A qualitative analysis of interprofessional primary care team members' perspectives. Journal of Interprofessional Care. 2019;**33**(6):836-838

[83] Morgan SE, Mosser A, Ahn S, Harrison TR, Wang J, Huang Q, et al. Developing and evaluating a team development intervention to support interdisciplinary teams. Journal of Clinical and Translational Science. 2021;**5**(e166):1-13. DOI: 10.1017/cts.2021.831

[84] Wong CH, Fu Y, Wong WH. Evaluation of healthcare information

systems: From evaluation models to evaluation approaches. Health Informatics Journal. 2013;**19**(2):83-99. DOI: 10.1177/1460458212449493

[85] Cohen SL, Senapati S, Gargiulo AR, Srouji SS, Tu FF, Solnik J, et al. Prospective evaluation of three different scoring systems for prediction of surgical complications after laparoscopic myomectomy. American Journal of Obstetrics and Gynecology. 2016;**214**(6):706.e1-706.e9. DOI: 10.1016/j.ajog.2016.01.180

[86] Neily J, Mills PD, Young-Xu Y, Carney BT, West P, Berger DH, et al. Association between implementation of a medical team training program and surgical mortality. JAMA. 2010;**304**(15):1693-1700. DOI: 10.1001/jama.2010.1506

[87] Murrells T, Ball J, Maben J, Ashworth M, Griffiths P, Nurse Forecasting Programme Project Team. Nursing workforce trends and their implications for patient care: A mixed-methods systematic review. Health Services and Delivery Research. 2016;**4**(6):1-234. DOI: 10.3310/hsdr04060

[88] Landrigan CP, Parry GJ, Bones CB, Hackbarth AD, Goldmann DA, Sharek PJ. Temporal trends in rates of patient harm resulting from medical care. New England Journal of Medicine. 2010;**363**(22):2124-2134. DOI: 10.1056/NEJMsa1004404

[89] Graupner C, Kimman ML, Mul S, Slok AHM, Claessens D, Kleijnen J, et al. Patient outcomes, patient experiences and process indicators associated with the routine use of patient-reported outcome measures (PROMs) in cancer care: A systematic review. Supportive Care in Cancer. 2021;**29**:573-593. DOI: 10.1007/s00520-020-05695-4

[90] Glickman SW, Boulding W, Manary M, Staelin R, Roe MT, Wolosin RJ, et al. Patient satisfaction and its relationship with clinical quality and inpatient mortality in acute myocardial infarction. Circulation: Cardiovascular Quality and Outcomes. 2010;**3**(2):188-195. DOI: 10.1161/CIRCOUTCOMES.109.900597

[91] Spaulding EM, Marvel FA, Jacob E, Rahman A, Hansen BR, Hanyok LA, et al. Interprofessional education and collaboration among healthcare students and professionals: A systematic review and call for action. Journal of Interprofessional Care. 2021;**35**(4):612-621. DOI: 10.1080/13561820.2019.1697214

[92] Bashshur RL, Howell JD, Krupinski EA, Harms KM, Bashshur N. The empirical foundations of telemedicine interventions in primary care. Telemedicine and e-Health. 2016;**22**(5):342-375

[93] Adler-Milstein J, Holmgren AJ, Kralovec P. Electronic health record data sharing: Characteristics of practices supporting high levels of information exchange. Annals of Internal Medicine. 2019;**170**(11):799-806

[94] Scott BK, Miller GT, Fonda SJ, Yeaw RE, Gaudaen JC, Pavliscsak HH, et al. Advanced digital health technologies for COVID-19 and future emergencies. Telemedicine and e-Health. 2020;**26**(10):1226-1233. DOI: 10.1089/tmj.2020.0140

[95] Morrice DJ, Bard JF, Koenig KM. Designing and scheduling a multi-disciplinary integrated practice unit for patient-centred care. Health Systems. 2020;**9**(4):293-316. DOI: 10.1080/20476965.2019.1569481

[96] Rosenthal MB, Friedberg MW, Singer SJ, Eastman D, Li Z,

Schneider EC, et al. Effect of a multipayer patient-centered medical home on health care utilization and quality. Annals of Internal Medicine. 2016;**165**(8):586-596

[97] Eppich WJ, Cheng A. Promoting Excellence and Reflective Learning in Simulation (PEARLS): Development and rationale for a blended approach to health care simulation debriefing. Simulation in Healthcare. 2015;**10**(2):106-115

[98] Burgess A, van Diggele C, Roberts C, Mellis C. Team-based learning: Design, facilitation and participation. BMC Medical Education. 2020, 2020;**20**(Suppl. 2):461. DOI: 10.1186/s12909-020-02287-y

[99] Considine J, Berry D, Allen J, Hewitt N, Oldland E, Sprogis SK, et al. Team-based learning in nursing education: A scoping review. Journal of Clinical Nursing. 2021;**30**(7-8):903-917. DOI: 10.1111/jocn.15599

[100] Roch G, Dubois C, Clarke SP. Organizational climate and hospital nurses' caring practices: A mixed-methods study. Research in Nursing & Health. 2014;**37**:229-240

[101] Archer J, Bower P, Gilbody S, Lovell K, Richards D, Gask L, et al. Collaborative care for depression and anxiety problems. Cochrane Database of Systematic Reviews. 2012;**10**(10):CD006525

[102] Rollman BL, Belnap BH, Mazumdar S, Houck PR, Zhu F, Gardner W, et al. A randomized trial to improve the quality of treatment for panic and generalized anxiety disorders in primary care. Archives of General Psychiatry. 2017;**69**(6):1330-1338

[103] Mlambo M, Silén C, Cormac McGrath C. Lifelong learning and nurses' continuing professional development, a metasynthesis of the literature. BMC Nursing. 2021;**20**:62. DOI: 10.1186/s12912-021-00579-2

[104] Bates DW, Saria S, Ohno-Machado L, Shah A, Escobar G. Big data in health care: Using analytics to identify and manage high-risk and high-cost patients. Health Affairs. 2014;**33**(7):1123-1131

[105] Padmanaban H. Navigating the complexity of regulations: Harnessing AI/ML for precise reporting. Journal of Artificial Intelligence General Science. 2024;**3**(1):49-61. DOI: 10.60087/jaigs.v3i1.65

[106] Carayon P, Wetterneck TB, Rivera-Rodriguez AJ, Hundt AS, Hoonakker P, Holden R, et al. Human factors systems approach to healthcare quality and patient safety. Applied Ergonomics. 2013;**45**(1):14-25

[107] Clarke L, Cameron C. The Key to R-E-S-P-E-C-T Is Human-Centred Design. Nursing Leadership (Tor Ont). 2022;**35**(2):44-48. DOI: 10.12927/cjnl.2022.26872

[108] Kyle MA, Emma-Louise Aveling E, Sara Singer S. A mixed methods study of change processes enabling effective transition to team-based care. Medical Care Research and Review. 2021;**78**(4):326-337. DOI: 10.1177/1077558719881854

[109] Rich E, Lipson D, Libersky J, Parchman M, Ladden MD, Kilo C. Organizing care for complex patients in the patient-centered medical home. Annals of Family Medicine. 2014;**12**(1):60-62

Chapter 5

Team Effectiveness in General Practice: Insights from the Norwegian Primary Healthcare Team Pilot

Birgit Abelsen and Anette Fosse

Abstract

This chapter provides insights into team effectiveness in general practice. It is based on a qualitative case study from five purposively recruited Norwegian general practices participating in a pilot for implementing primary healthcare teams. To assess team effectiveness, 41 individual and group interviews were performed in the practices. The data production and the analysis were guided by Hackman's team effectiveness model. Five overarching themes were identified: teamwork nature, buy-in, macro-team leadership, individual satisfaction, and performance outcome. Despite variation in the organizational context, the informants at four of five of the practices agreed that functional teamwork produced good and relevant results—primarily for the patients, as well as largely for themselves as it increased job satisfaction. The study shows that becoming real and effective micro- or macro-teams involves extensive, targeted, and time-consuming change work. Actual change requires leadership, buy-in, and a significant effort linked to structuring the teamwork. The results raise the question of whether it is a sensible use of resources to scale up and spread primary healthcare teams to all general practices in Norway. Management training as part of specialist training for all general practitioners to acquire the competence to lead effective micro-teams could be beneficial for teamwork development.

Keywords: interprofessional team, teamwork, team effectiveness, micro-team, macro-team, primary healthcare, general practice, implementation

1. Introduction

Interprofessional primary healthcare teams (PHTs) are promoted as necessary for handling the complexity of contemporary and future healthcare provision and as essential for the ability to provide high-quality and safe healthcare [1–3]. Schmutz et al. [4] found that teamwork has a positive relationship to performance, regardless of the characteristics of the team or task, and concluded that healthcare organizations should recognize the value of teamwork and emphasize approaches that maintain and improve teamwork for the benefit of patients.

While the assumption that complex health issues are managed better by teams is widely endorsed, the implementation of such teamwork can be challenging [5–10]. An overview of reviews of interprofessional collaboration in primary healthcare highlighted that most barriers and facilitators were reported at the organizational and inter-individual levels [11]. In general practice, the most frequently reported barriers to well-functioning teamwork between general practitioners (GPs) and nurses were at the system level (e.g., inadequate reimbursement policies for nurses' services) and at the inter-individual level (e.g., traditional hierarchies, ideological differences in practice and cultural perception of care leading to power struggles, and difficulties regarding professional identity). The most frequently reported facilitators at the organizational level included tools for team communication (e.g., regular meetings, open channels of communication, and use of technologies) and close physical proximity between professionals. At the inter-individual level, the definition of roles and responsibilities and the acceptance of other professionals' views, competences and practices, and shared leadership were reported. At the individual level, a positive attitude and interest in interprofessional collaboration was identified [12, 13].

The effectiveness of teamwork may vary according to the context [14, 15]. The importance of studying the effectiveness of a team in the specific context in which the teamwork is taking place is emphasized, because of the effect of the context on team processes, psychosocial traits (e.g., cohesion and norms), and task design [16]. A review of interventions to improve team effectiveness found that most studies researched different acute hospital settings and pointed out that less evidence is available about team effectiveness in primary care settings, including general practice [17].

Our study aimed to investigate team effectiveness in interprofessional primary healthcare teams in general practice. The study was carried out in connection with a pilot project introducing interprofessional PHTs in Norwegian general practice. The pilot is part of an international teamwork trend in general practice. The descriptions and evaluations of international initiatives show a diversity of organizational methods and results [18–21]. The heterogeneity in health systems justify national pilots and associated evaluations in individual countries ahead of eventual whole-system changes.

This study provides contextual insights into team effectiveness. The fact that we are studying a change process that seeks to establish teamwork means that the study probably uncovers aspects that are different from those that would be found in a study of team effectiveness in an established teamwork structure. The study finds that effective teamwork is not necessarily achieved even when both effort and interest are present. Based on the findings, this chapter recommends strategies that can facilitate the implementation of interprofessional teamwork in general practice.

2. Theoretical framework

Health services research has focused on identifying the characteristics of effective teams and developing instruments for measuring team effectiveness [16, 22]. Team effectiveness can be measured by looking at objective outcomes (e.g., quality of care) or subjective outcomes (e.g., effectiveness as perceived by team members) [23]. The theoretical framework guiding the current study is Hackman's model for assessing team effectiveness [24, 25]. The underpinning idea is that team effectiveness depends on three main outcomes: acceptable performance output, the growth and well-being of the team members, and the viability of the team. Performance outputs may include factors such as patient satisfaction, quality of care, adherence to clinical guidelines, and efficient utilization of resources. Performance output assessments are subjective and are carried out either by the team members themselves (as in this study) or by patients experiencing the teamwork. To achieve the outcomes, the model identifies six conditions: the performing unit is a real team; the team has a compelling direction or purpose; there is a strong and supportive structure; there is a conducive and supportive context; there is the right mix of competent and committed members; and there is competent coaching. Further, team effectiveness is seen as a function of three overarching processes: collective effort, use of knowledge and skills, and a strategy for carrying out the teamwork. The model acknowledges that the outputs of the team, in turn, become inputs for the next cycle of team performance. The outputs provide feedback to the team and influence future inputs, shaping the team's ongoing effectiveness.

3. Study context

Since 2001, Norway has had a patient list system for general practice. This system gives each of the 5.4 million Norwegian citizens the right to be registered with a regular GP; only a minimal number of people opt out [26]. The primary objective of the patient list system is to secure access and continuity of care. Regular GPs provide consultations with their listed patients and coordinate the care of these patients within the healthcare system while also serving as gatekeepers to secondary care and sickness benefits. The GP service is a municipal service. Most GPs are self-employed and operate under an individual agreement with the municipality. A minority of GPs, particularly in rural areas, are employed and work in general practices owned by the municipality.

Over the years, the general population has been very satisfied with the patient list system [27]. In 2022, a regular GP had, on average, 1040 patients on his or her list [28]. GPs typically work in quite small practices alongside other regular GPs (mean: 5.0, interquartile range: [3–6]) [29], and it is uncommon for practices to include other professionals except medical assistants. Thus, interprofessional teamwork inside general practices is less developed in Norway than in many other European countries [30].

The Norwegian Directorate of Health initiated a primary healthcare team (PHT) pilot in the period April 2018–March 2023. The aim was to explore whether a PHT provided a better service for patients than the usual GP scheme. General practices were expanded with nurses, and PHTs included regular GPs, nurses, and medical assistants. PHTs were expected to offer home visits, quality, availability, continuity, and safe services and to work systematically and proactively with target patient groups such as weak demanders and patients with large and complex needs in four main categories: patients with chronic diseases, patients with mental health problems and/or substance abuse problems, frail elderly, and patients with developmental disorders/disabilities [31]. No further directions were given for how the teamwork was to be carried out.

The PHT pilot included 17 self-recruited general practices, each of which included between three and 17 regular GPs, between one and six nurses, and between two and six medical assistants. Each general practice comprised a macro-team and several

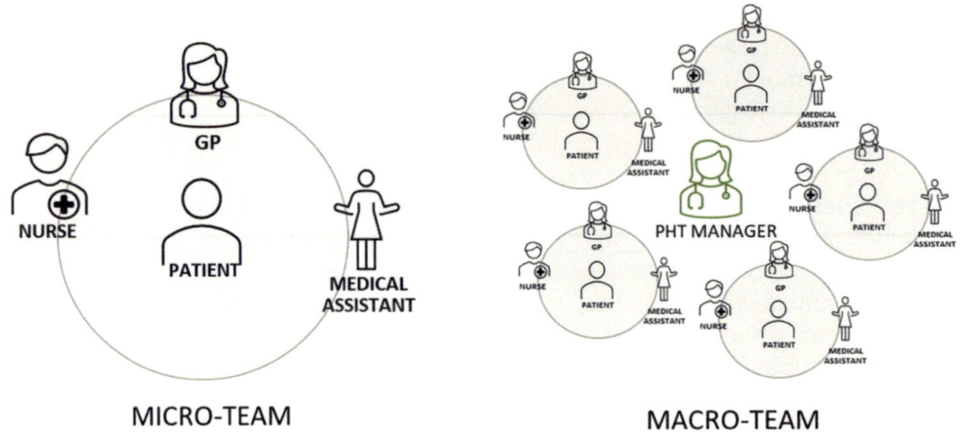

Figure 1.
The micro-team and macro-team.

micro-teams—a common structure, particularly in US models of primary healthcare teams [32–35]. The macro-team included all professionals working in the practice and was led by a PHT manager (one of the GPs). The micro-teams were formed based on each individual GP's listed patients and were led by the respective GPs. Normatively, a micro-team was expected to include the GP, a nurse, and a medical assistant (see **Figure 1**). As part of the pilot, the PHT managers were offered management training corresponding to 30 study credits.

The pilot provided funding for the nurse resource in the approximate ratio of one nurse to three regular GPs. Nurses were employed with fixed salaries. The regular GP scheme is funded based on activity with approximately 30 percent capitation, and only the GPs' work is financed. For the pilot, two funding models were available: the activity-based model and a block funding model. Patient co-payment was the same in both models. Within the activity-based model, the GPs claimed fees and patient co-payments as normal. The nurses claimed fees and patient co-payments for the services they provided, with around 50 percent of their salary funded by a fixed allowance from the state. The block funding model relies on risk-adjusted capitation as the main source of funding for the whole practice. Patient co-payments and payments by result indicators make up a small portion of the funding in this model.

By the end of June 2023, 12 percent of the listed patients in the 17 pilot practices had had contact with the PHT [36].

This case study is part of a greater multi-method evaluation study following the pilot [36, 37]. Author BA is an experienced healthcare researcher. Author AF has been working as a GP for 30 years. We share an interest in general practice and in how it can be developed to meet the population's increasing and changing needs for healthcare.

4. Research question

We sought to answer the following research question: How do team members subjectively assess the team effectiveness of the micro- and macro-teams implemented in their general practice?

5. Methods

5.1 Sample

Five general practices with different profiles and staffing were purposively included in this interview study. **Table 1** sums up some of the relevant characteristics of the selected practices. We aimed for variation in the choice of funding model, ownership, staff size and mixture, whether they had nurses before they joined the pilot, the fee-generation among the nurses, and geographical placement and size. The table also shows the number of interviews conducted for the present study and the proportion of the staff that participated.

Three of the practices were funded on the activity-based model, and two had block funding. The number of GPs varied from four to ten, and the practices had between two and six medical assistants. Two of the practices had previously had nurses. In the pilot, each of the five practices engaged between one and three PHT nurses. The practices were in different parts of Norway and covered urban and rural areas. The interviewees were PHT managers (5), GPs (21), PHT nurses (8), other nurses (7), and medical assistants (11).

5.2 Qualitative interviews

The data for our study were collected 4 years after the start of the pilot. Based on Hackman's model for assessing team effectiveness, we designed interview guides with the aim of exploring team effectiveness in the micro-and macro-teams in the five practices. To prepare themselves, the interviewees received a thematic interview guide with key topics in advance (see **Table 2**). The interviewer used a more detailed, structured interview guide with specific questions, making sure that all interviews followed the same order and covered all the themes.

In May and June 2022, 41 structured interviews were performed, five on videocalls and the rest face-to-face in the practices. The PHT managers, GPs, and PHT nurses were interviewed individually, while the other health professionals were interviewed together in groups of two to five participants. The interviews lasted on average 57 minutes (median: 50, min/max: 16/75). They were audio-recorded and transcribed verbatim.

5.3 Analysis

Data analysis of the transcripts was performed with thematic analysis according to Braun and Clarke [38]. We were inspired by an abductive approach in qualitative research [39] theoretically informed by Hackman's model for team effectiveness. Both authors read the material thoroughly and worked together to reach consensus in interpretation of themes in the qualitative data. We generated and negotiated initial codes and text extracts representing the participants' experiences with introducing teamwork in macro- and micro-teams and collated these into potential themes. The analysis was performed stepwise; first with five overarching themes being named (see **Table 2**) and then with the material within each practice being analyzed considering the five overarching themes. In an iterative process, we reviewed the sub-themes considering the research question and the coded extracts, named them, and finally condensed and synthesized the extracts into analytic text. Our preconceptions were mixed when it came to the PHT pilot, leading to a fruitful balance in our approach to the analysis and discussion. The stepwise analysis of text from each practice made

		General practices				
		Practice 1	Practice 2	Practice 3	Practice 4	Practice 5
Funding model		Activity-based model	Block funding model	Activity-based model	Block funding model	Activity-based model
Practice ownership		Private	Public	Private	Private	Public
Size of municipality (No. of inhabitants)		[20,000–50,000]	[5000–20,000>	> 0.5 million	> 0.5 million	[5000–20,000>
Municipal centrality		Semirural	Rural	Urban	Urban	Rural
Nurse new with PHT		No	No	Yes	Yes	No
Fee-generating contacts with nurses		60% joint consultations, 17% sole consultations	53% home visits, 33% sole consultations	56% sole consultations, 8% basic contacts	55% sole consultations, 23% basic contacts	58% sole consultations, 36% basic contacts
No. of practice staff	No. of GPs	10	6	4	5	10
	No. of PHT nurses	3	2	2	1	2
	No. of other nurses		4			4
	Medical assistants and other personnel	7	2	4	2	2
No. of individual interviews	GPs	7	4	4	4	7
	PHT nurses	2	2	1	1	2
No. of group interviews/ informants	Nurses, medical assistants and other personnel	1/4	2/4	1/3	1 / 2	1 / 5

Table 1.
Key characteristics of the five selected general practices.

PHT managers, GPs, and nurses	Medical assistants
• PHT in this general practice • Results and benefits of PHT • The importance of PHT for patients • Teamwork skills • Teamwork challenges • Freedom of action in the teamwork • Teamwork effects • Losses associated with the teamwork • Team size and associated expertise • Need and opportunity for skills development • PHT management • Working methods within the general practice • Self-evaluation of the teamwork	• PHT in this general practice • The medical assistants' role in the teamwork • Results and benefits of PHT • The importance of PHT for patients • Collaboration with the GPs • Collaboration with nurse(s) • New challenges with teamwork • Losses associated with the teamwork • Team size and associated expertise • Need and opportunity for skills development • PHT management • Self-evaluation of the teamwork

Table 2.
Thematic interview guide to interviews with PHT managers, GPs, nurses, and medical assistants.

it possible to compare and discuss similarities and differences between the different funding and organizational contexts. The five PHT managers were invited to read through and comment on the text, resulting in minor adjustments.

5.4 Ethics

The Norwegian Agency for Shared Services in Education and Research was notified of the study (#405955) and ensured that the planned data processing was in accordance with data protection legislation. Ahead of the interview, all participants received the interview guide and information about the study. Agreement to take part was implicit through attendance at the interview.

6. Findings

The analysis identified five overarching themes capturing the informants' team effectiveness assessments: teamwork nature, buy-in, macro-team leadership, individual satisfaction, and performance outcome (see **Table 3**).

6.1 Teamwork nature

The nature of the teamwork varied greatly between the practices. At Practice 1 (P1), the teamwork was based on formalized patient follow-up procedures. It was mainly carried out in joint consultations led by the nurse, with the GP attending the final phase. The informants said that they had worked hard on developing the procedures and on finding a common way of working. The nurse and the GP communicated electronically in real time during the consultation, and the GP had to find time to participate in the final phase. There were no formal meetings between the individual nurse and GP other than these consultations in which the patient also

Themes	General practices				
	Practice 1	Practice 2	Practice 3	Practice 4	Practice 5
Teamwork nature	Well-structured macro teamwork. Unified way of micro-team working and generally structured patient follow-up procedures. Most of the nurses' fee generation stems from joint consultations with the GP.	Well-structured macro teamwork. Flexibility but largely a unified and highly coordinated way of working in micro-teams. Most of the nurses' fee generation stems from home visits.	Some structure in the macro teamwork. No unified way of micro-team working. Most of the nurses' fee generation stems from their sole consultations with patients.	Some structure in the macro teamwork. No unified way of micro-team working. Most of the nurses' fee generation stems from her consultations with patients and basic contacts with patients and others. One PHT nurse is partly doing medical assistant work.	No structuring of the macro teamwork. No unified way of micro-team working. Most of the nurses' fee generation stems from their sole consultations with patients and basic contacts with patients and others.
Buy-In	Strong among all the GPs and nurses. Varied among the medical assistants.	Strong among all the professional groups.	Weak among most of the GPs. Varied among the nurses. Strong among the medical assistants.	Varied among the GPs.	Varied among the GPs. Strong among the nurses. Indifference among the other professionals.
Macro-team leadership	Firm and clear. The PHT manager is referred to as a very good leader by fellow workers.	Present, clear, enthusiastic, and inclusive.	Partly absent. Challenging to conduct consensus management when consensus is lacking among the GPs.	Partly absent.	Completely absent during the Covid-19 pandemic. Distance leadership of the practice is also a negative factor.
Individual satisfaction	High and consistent among the GPs and nurses. Varied among the medical assistants.	High and consistent among all the professional groups.	Varied among both the GPs and the nurses. Strong among the medical assistants.	Varied among the GPs. Strong in the nurse. Low among the medical assistants.	Varied among the GPs. Strong among the PHT nurses. Indifference among the other professionals.
Performance output	Health benefits for patients. Increased job satisfaction.	Health benefits for patients. Increased job satisfaction.	Increased quality of patient care. Increased job satisfaction.	Increased quality of patient care. PHT has made it possible for the GPs to be salaried and use time on macro-team meetings without economic loss. This is highly valued among the GPs.	Varied opinions.

Table 3.
Overarching themes in team members' evaluation of PHT effectiveness in the five selected general practices.

DOI: http://dx.doi.org/10.5772/intechopen.1004545

participated. The nurses had a weekly meeting among themselves and a meeting with the PHT manager to discuss PHT-related topics. The PHT manager and the GPs also had regular meetings. The informants spoke of these meetings as being important for the development of procedures and the common way of team working. The working method was continuously evaluated and adjusted. The GPs agreed that they were the ones who controlled the patients' access to the PHT and that there had to be a clear plan for the team follow-up of individual patients. The use of formalized procedures was seen as an assurance for high-quality and equal services. The GPs agreed that a certain degree of individual difference between them was fine but that this had to be balanced so that the patients received equal services. The nurses reported that they had the same approach to the micro-team working with all the GPs.

The work at Practice 2 (P2) was described as team-based, with several nurses having been on the staff long before the PHT pilot was established. Participation in the pilot had provided a larger nurse resource and a more targeted use of this resource. Previously, a nurse had had largely the same function as a medical assistant. In the PHT, all the nurses took on nursing tasks that demanded more competence. Two nurses (the PHT nurses) mostly worked in the PHT. The other nurses worked in the PHT as a minor part of their jobs. As part of the PHT, the nurses followed up patients, according to agreed procedures, in their own consultations, either in the patient's home or in the practice. The PHT nurses had weekly meetings with the individual GPs in which current patient follow-up in the micro-teams was discussed. The whole staff participated in daily 10–15-minute morning meetings and often in short informal "debriefs" when the phone lines had closed for the day. The informants agreed that they had developed a clear, common structure and way of micro-team working.

At Practice 3 (P3), Practice 4 (P4), and Practice 5 (P5), no manifest structures or common teamworking methods had been developed. Most of the nurses' fee-generation stemmed from their own contact with patients. In P4 and P5, a high proportion was from basic contact (not directly PHT-related) with patients and others, suggesting that the nurses did tasks that the medical assistants could have done just as well. At P3 and P4, there were weekly whole-staff meetings with PHT themes on the agenda. However, although patient follow-up procedures were developed on paper and it was decided that there should also be weekly meetings between each individual GP and the nurse, the micro-teamwork was carried out to a varying degree. The GPs often occupied the meeting time with patient consultations. At P5, there was no established meeting structure or framework whatsoever to support the teamwork. The nurses at all the three general practices spoke of great variation in their micro-teamwork with the individual GPs: with some GPs, it worked very well; with some, it worked less well, and with some, there was no teamwork at all.

6.2 Buy-in

Buy-in also differed between the practices. At P1, the GPs and nurses unanimously expressed great commitment and buy-in to the PHT. They had transformed into the PHT with great desire. The medical assistants did not, however, express the same buy-in. They believed that they should have been more involved in the teamwork. Several of the other informants said that they had tried to bring out the medical assistants' important macro-team role in ensuring good patient flow, communication, and interaction. The PHT manager said that they had been concerned with creating ownership and team spirit among all the staff. He emphasized that the PHT was a joint assignment:

> *We are explicit that we must be something more. We must be something extra. And what can you contribute to this extra [...] be clear that we work as a team. We need your participation and your commitment to this team, so that the team is not a manager and some workers, it is a shared responsibility. (PHT leader, P1)*

At P2, all the informants expressed strong team affiliation. Several said that their sense of ownership had developed over time. Many pointed to the PHT manager's commitment and targeted work to involve everyone as an important factor for team buy-in.

At P3, the informants talked about many replacements among the GPs and an accompanying challenge in creating team ownership among the new GPs and GP locums. The PHT manager explained the other GPs' lack of ownership by saying that they did not experience the same degree of quality and relief in workload from the PHT as he did himself and that they paid too much attention to their own earnings. The other GPs largely confirmed this explanation. One GP was explicit that it was out of the question to "pay" nurses for work that she felt she had the capacity to do herself. The situation was nevertheless experienced as a dilemma, as the GP also saw the professional need for team follow-up among vulnerable listed patients. The nurses and medical assistants expressed a clear team commitment. They talked about the difficulties in creating buy-in among new GPs who had more than enough to do with getting to know their listed patients. The new GPs were not sufficiently informed about the PHT and did not know what to do to become part of it.

At P4, the informants described varying degrees of buy-in between the professions. The PHT manager believed that this had to do with several changes. The practice had expanded, with two new GPs, and both the initial PHT manager and the initial nurse had left. The GPs generally expressed satisfaction with the teamwork, but the new nurse said she lacked a plan for how to work. The medical assistants felt they were sidelined and not heard. They had not been given any special team role, and tasks that they enjoyed had been lost to the nurse.

The PHT manager at P5 spoke of a wide range in the GPs' views of the PHT—from completely passive and uninterested to enthusiastic and committed. This was confirmed in the individual interviews with the GPs. The nurses said that it had been challenging with an experienced GP staff who had no desire to change their way of working. During the PHT pilot, new GPs and younger GP locums had come in, making teamwork easier because the newcomers were more used to working with nurses. The medical assistants felt barely involved in the PHT. When they, and some of the GPs, talked about the PHT, they meant the PHT nurses. When asked why, one of the medical assistants replied:

> *In other practices it seems like they're all involved – it is us in the practice who are the PHT. Whereas here we have always perceived [the PHT] as them [the PHT nurses]. [...] So, I feel there is something we've missed. (Medical assistant, P5)*

6.3 Macro-team leadership

At P1 and P2, all the informants spoke very positively about the PHT managers' leadership. At P1, the PHT manager was referred to as a very capable leader, with great drive and commitment to the PHT. His macro-team leadership was foregrounded as being decisive in what they had achieved. However, several informants added that the leadership had a good foundation, in that some of the other staff members had a similar commitment and buy-in and that the staff had allowed itself to be led. At P2, all the informants highlighted the PHT manager as committed, inclusive, positive, and solution-oriented. Her clear objective was that everyone should take part in the teamwork. At both practices, it was pointed out that there was a big difference between the PHT managers before and after they had attended management training. The management training gave the PHT managers both the competence and the authority to lead.

The PHT manager at P3 considered himself too old for management training and was unsure of its usefulness in a practice with a flat structure. The PHT manager believed that his management had to be based on consensus, and as consensus was lacking, it was difficult for him to lead. The staff experienced his leadership somewhat differently. The GPs mainly thought that the PHT manager had done a good leadership job. The nurses pointed to a lack of time for leadership in a hectic everyday life.

The PHT manager at P4 had also completed management training. However, he found it challenging to take over the leadership role in addition to handling a full patient list. The GPs were divided in their views of his leadership. The medical assistants and the nurse said that they experienced too little leadership and missed being followed up.

The PHT manager at P5 had also participated in management training. However, his assessment was that there had been a clear deficit in PHT management. For a long period, his resources had been used for the municipality's handling of the Covid-19 pandemic. The other informants experienced a clear absence of leadership of both the PHT and the practice. Since the municipality had taken over the administration of the practice a few years earlier, a municipal health manager had formally managed the practice on a part-time basis. This person was not regularly present at the practice, was not a GP, and, according to the PHT manager, lacked the legitimacy to lead the GPs. As municipal employees, the nurses found that it was the municipal health manager who controlled their working hours and work content. During the Covid-19 pandemic, it had been more important for the municipality that they did other tasks than PHT work.

6.4 Individual satisfaction

At P1, all the GPs and nurses said that they were satisfied with the teamworking. At P2, all the informants expressed that they enjoyed teamworking and experienced it as meaningful. In both practices, the informants said that teamwork provided a greater professional community than before. Several GPs pointed out that it was nice not to be so alone with the patients as they had previously been. The teamwork made them do a better job, and this brought them great joy. Both PHT managers saw it as a great privilege for the practices and the local community to be part of the pilot.

At the other three practices, individual satisfaction with PHT varied widely both within and between the professional groups. At P4, one nurse had her last day when the interview was done. She had resigned because she felt that her expertise was being misused as a lot of her time had been spent doing medical assistant tasks. At P5, the medical assistants talked about a frustrating work situation with a heavy workload and low job satisfaction. At the time of the interview, one medical assistant was on long-term sick leave, and another had got a new job at a hospital.

6.5 Performance output

At P1, P2, P3, and P4, almost all the informants had concrete stories about individual patients who had greatly benefited from their teamwork. The informants pointed out that the teamwork (when it was functioning) gave higher quality, more of an overview, a more stable patient follow-up process, and time to explore unclear issues. They also talked about patients expressing satisfaction with team follow-up. The systematic approach facilitated by the procedures contributed to reducing errors and improving workflow. At P1, the informants believed that the PHT also gave a larger production than before.

At P1, P2, and P4, the informants were most definite in their judgment that the teamwork not only increased the quality of patient care but also gave patients better health and well-being. At P3, several informants pointed out that team follow-up was particularly useful also for their listed population, where many had an immigrant background, were economically poor, had a low education level, and for various reasons did not follow up their own illness(es) well enough.

In the case of P4, the choice of the block funding model had enabled the GPs to switch from variable income to having a fixed salary. Several of the GPs were satisfied with this. The funding model had given them the opportunity to hold meetings and follow up patients without being worried about finances.

In P5, the results of PHT were assessed differently within and between the professional groups. The nurses and some GPs talked about positive results for the patients in the same way as the informants at the other practices, but there were also informants among the GPs and medical assistants who either thought it was difficult to assess the results because the PHT objective was unclear or believed that the PHT had not brought about any change whatsoever.

Although the quality of patient care and the health-related results for the patients were noted as the most important, many of the informants at P1, P2, P3, and P4 pointed out that the teamwork provided job satisfaction and security for themselves. It also gave them someone to share their joys with—someone who knew the patient and, for example, knew the effort that had been put in to get to the position where they could help someone who was mentally ill. The PHT had changed their attitudes and the respect they had for each other. It had increased their understanding and appreciation of everyone's contribution. The impact of the PHT on job satisfaction was mentioned to a lesser extent by the informants at P5.

7. Discussion

This study shows that becoming real and effective micro- or macro-teams in general practice involves extensive, targeted, and time-consuming development and change work. In addition to clear leadership, actual change requires buy-in and a significant effort linked to structuring the teamwork. The organizational context for teamwork, which is most clearly reflected in the informants' stories about teamwork nature, buy-in, leadership, and individual satisfaction, varied widely between the five practices. P1 and P2 largely fulfilled the criteria, conditions, and processes set by Hackman [24, 25] to create team effectiveness. The other three practices (P3, P4, and P5) had been less successful in this. However, despite variations in the organizational context, the informants at P1, P2, P3, and P4 agreed that functional teamwork produced good and relevant results, primarily for the patients as well as largely for themselves as it increased their job satisfaction. These results are in line with findings in other studies [4, 15, 34, 40]. The stories told by the informants at P1 and P2 indicate an increase over time in their ability to collaborate. Role clarification and a reasonable distribution of labor in both the macro- and the micro-teams ensured that different skills were used well. This teamwork viability was present to a lesser extent in P3, P4, and P5. Important reasons for this seem to be turnover, especially among the GPs, and a lack of both macro- and micro-team leadership. It cannot be ruled out that the reason for turnover was a lack of success in changing to teamwork. Lack of structure, leadership, and support had a negative impact on the assessments of team effectiveness; for example, the team members to a lesser extent had a common perception of the purpose of the teamwork, and the distribution of responsibility and tasks was to varying degrees agreed upon in the macro-teams. The negative impacts of turnover and a lack of leadership are known, from other studies, to hamper teamwork [7, 9, 41, 42].

The patient list system set natural frames for the micro-teams, and the medical assistants seemed to have no function or enhanced role in these teams. This contrasts with the way in which the micro-teams were normatively described as part of the pilot [31] and with findings from other studies [33, 34]. However, the medical assistants had an important role and contribution to the macro-team and the functioning of the practices. Our study shows that a micro-team (i.e., a GP and nurse) can function well even if the practice does not achieve a unified way of micro-teamworking. However, the fact that certain micro-teams function less effectively reduces the overall team effectiveness in the practice. The informants' descriptions indicate that different aspects determined the micro-team practice. The GP's buy-in was important, and what seemed to be decisive was whether the GP took the expected leadership and managed the micro-team for the benefit of their listed patients in the target group. The GP's experience was also important. New GPs needed time to get to know their listed patients and find out who might benefit from team-based follow-up. In addition, it seemed that new GPs were not sufficiently socialized into PHTs and only partly understood the concept, which is related to a lack of macro-team leadership, buy-in, and support at the practice. On the other hand, some young GPs connected more easily to teamwork because they were used to it from hospital settings, while some old GPs wanted to continue in their usual way of working.

Hackman's normative model for assessing team effectiveness (1987) has been a suitable theoretical starting point for our study. However, the model is not specifically developed for assessing teamwork in general practice. It emphasizes the importance of real teams as a condition for team effectiveness but does not pay particular attention to aspects related to turnover in teams. Turnover was a significant issue at three of the practices (P3-P5) in our study. Turnover, especially among GPs, probably creates some unique challenges in a patient list system. It takes time for new GPs to gain an overview of their listed patients' needs. At the same time, the Norwegian list system is largely built on self-employment and individual contracts between GPs and the municipalities, which promotes GPs' autonomy and not teamwork. For studies in general practice, it may be appropriate to add team stability as a condition for creating team effectiveness.

The funding models (activity-based or block funding) did not in general seem to have a decisive impact on teamwork effectiveness. This might relate to self-selection into the funding models. However, the fact that teamwork could give a lower income to self-employed GPs funded on the activity-based model was highlighted as an explanatory factor for the lack of interest in teamwork among informants at P3, while the opportunities that came with the choice of the block funding model were highlighted by the informants at P4 as something that enhanced teamwork. Similar perceptions have been identified in previous studies [42, 43]. The fact that our informants did not place more emphasis on financial aspects may have to do with the fact that Hackman's model does not include these aspects. This could be a potential weakness with the model when studying team effectiveness in a general practice model based primarily on self-employed GPs.

Tuckman's [44] sequential stages of development for groups solving tasks together (forming, storming, norming, and performing) is an alternative theoretical framework that can help make sense of team development. In the forming phase, boundaries for work tasks and relationships are tested at the same time as the individuals adjust to management, other team members, and the existing system. The storming phase is characterized by resistance and often conflict, linked to team influence and expected involvement. In the norming phase, resistance is overcome, the content of the collaboration and cohesion develops, and new standards, roles, and trust are established. In the performing phase, the structures are in place and support the tasks to be performed. Our findings suggest that at the time of the interviews, the five practices were in different phases. P1 and P2 had probably reached the performing phase, while it is likely that P3, P4, and P5 were still in the forming phase, mainly due to turnover and an absence of leadership. Awareness of Tuckman's four stages could be useful for studies on teamwork implementation in GP practices. Our study demonstrates that moving from one stage to the next does not happen automatically.

A strength of this study is that we interviewed almost all the health professionals at the practices and that the interviews were structured. Participation in the pilot was based on self-selection of the practices. There is reason to assume that at the participating practices, there was a genuine interest, among at least some of the staff, in bringing about a change to a more team-based way of working. Even though both time and interest have been present, our findings show that effective teamwork has not necessarily been achieved.

In their systematic literature review, Buljac-Samardzic et al. [17] show that studies on improving team functioning in healthcare focus on four types of intervention: training, tools, organizational (re)design, and programs. Programs refer to combinations of different interventions. Although the review mostly covers studies conducted in hospitals, the interventions seem relevant in connection with an eventual scaling-up and spread of PHT in Norwegian general practice. Our study shows that the management training offered to the PHT managers as part of the pilot had a positive impact on the development of teamwork, on both the macro and the micro levels. This could be a selection effect. On the other hand, it suggests that the PHT management training should be maintained. Our findings indicate that there will also be benefits in management training for all GPs so that they can acquire competence to lead effective microteams. This can, for example, be part of the specialist training in general practice.

Further, our findings indicate that the practices that participated in the PHT pilot have each spent a lot of time developing procedures for the team-based follow-up of different target patient groups. As part of the scaling-up and spread, such procedures should be standardized at national level with associated instruction manuals, including possibilities for sensible local adjustments [45]. Several of the practices in the PHT pilot have used information technology to carry out efficient, systematic searches of the patient lists to identify residents in the target groups who could benefit from team-based follow-up. This could develop into standard procedures. Both our study and others show that clear structures to ensure communication in the team are extremely important. Coombs et al. [32] find that the use of huddles (structured, brief, routine (multiple times a day), and face to-face communication between all members of a team) is both common and effective.

Organizational (re)design focuses on intervening in structures, which will consequently improve team functioning. Norwegian general practice is largely based on self-employment and individual contracts between each GP and the municipality through the general GP scheme system. Most GPs are organized into group practices. It is currently not an option for the municipality and a group-based practice to establish a contract on broader group services. Structural change that provides opportunities to enter into collective agreements on team-based services could support the development of teamwork to a greater extent. The interventions we have pointed to could form a program to support the further development and eventual scaling-up and spread of structured teamwork in Norwegian general practice.

8. Conclusion

Our findings indicate that well-functioning PHTs will be able to provide patients with good-quality primary care and that those who work in well-functioning teams are likely to experience increased job satisfaction. Well-functioning teams require leadership, buy-in, and a significant effort linked to structuring the teamwork and thus are resource-demanding. At general practices that are unable to create this type of team effectiveness, the positive results for patients and healthcare personnel are less likely. Based on our findings, we assume that on a large scale, there will be practices that will not succeed in becoming effective teams. There is also reason to believe that GPs in some practices will not be interested in teamwork at all. Our findings raise the question of whether it is a sensible use of resources to scale up and spread PHT to all general practices in Norway. The danger of a full-scale implementation of PHT is that the allocation of resources to this kind of teamwork might be a waste and create larger differences in the population's health service provision and associated health outcomes. On the other hand, knowing the many benefits of effective teamwork, it is important to look for strategies that can facilitate a stepwise full-scale implementation. Our study shows that it is important to have time and expertise for overall management of the macro team at the GP practice. However, it appears that micro-teams can function well regardless of the nature of the macro-team. Specialist training in general practice may be a favorable arena for providing GPs with expertise in the management of micro-teams. A low-threshold facilitation of micro-teams may give an opportunity for individual GPs and other health personnel to experience the benefits and challenges of teamwork.

Acknowledgements

Margrete Gaski participated in the study planning. She died in May 2022 and is therefore not included among the authors. The authors are very grateful to Margrete for her contribution. They would also like to thank the five participating general practices for all their help with arranging the interviews and the interviewees for sharing their views and experiences. The authors are members of the research team that evaluated the primary healthcare team pilot in Norway. The pilot was initiated by the Norwegian Directorate of Health (NDH), and they also funded the evaluation. The

NDH had no role in the design of the study, the collection, analysis, and interpretation of data, or the writing of this manuscript. The publication charges for this article have been funded by a grant from the publication fund of UiT the Arctic University of Norway.

Conflict of interest

The authors declare no conflict of interest.

Author details

Birgit Abelsen* and Anette Fosse
Department of Community Health, Norwegian Centre for Rural Medicine, UiT the Arctic University of Norway, Tromsø, Norway

*Address all correspondence to: birgit.abelsen@uit.no

References

[1] OECD. Realising the Potential of Primary Health Care. Paris: OECD; 2020

[2] Rosen MA, Diaz Granados D, Dietz AS, Benishek LE, Thompson D, Pronovost PJ, et al. Teamwork in healthcare: Key discoveries enabling safer, high-quality care. The American Psychologist. 2018;**73**(4):433-450. DOI: 10.1037/amp0000298

[3] WHO. The World Health Report 2008 - Primary Health Care: Now more than Ever. Geneva: WHO; 2008

[4] Schmutz JB, Meier LL, Manser T. How effective is teamwork really? The relationship between teamwork and performance in healthcare teams: A systematic review and meta-analysis. BMJ Open. 2019;**9**(9):e028280. DOI: 10.1136/bmjopen-2018-028280

[5] Bonciani M, Schäfer W, Barsanti S, Heinemann S, Groenewegen PP. The benefits of co-location in primary care practices: The perspectives of general practitioners and patients in 34 countries. BMC Health Services Research. 2018;**18**(1):132. DOI: 10.1186/s12913-018-2913-4

[6] Freund T, Everett C, Griffiths P, Hudon C, Naccarella L, Laurant M. Skill mix, roles and remuneration in the primary care workforce: Who are the healthcare professionals in the primary care teams across the world? International Journal of Nursing Studies. 2015;**52**(3):727-743. DOI: 10.1016/j.ijnurstu.2014.11.014

[7] Hall P. Interprofessional teamwork: Professional cultures as barriers. Journal of Interprofessional Care. 2005;**19**(Suppl 1):188-196. DOI: 10.1080/13561820500081745

[8] Kringos D, Boerma W, van der Zee J, Groenewegen P. Europe's strong primary care systems are linked to better population health but also to higher health spending. Health Affairs. 2013;**32**(4):686-694. DOI: 10.1377/hlthaff.2012.1242

[9] O'Sullivan M, Cullen W, MacFarlane A. Primary care teams in Ireland: A qualitative mapping review of Irish grey and published literature. Irish Journal of Medical Science. 2015;**184**(1):69-73. DOI: 10.1007/s11845-014-1128-x

[10] Sibbald SL, Misra V, da Silva M, Licskai C. A framework to support the progressive implementation of integrated team-based care for the management of COPD: A collective case study. BMC Health Services Research. 2022;**22**(1):420. DOI: 10.1186/s12913-022-07785-x

[11] Rawlinson C, Carron T, Cohidon C, Arditi C, Hong QN, Pluye P, et al. An overview of reviews on interprofessional collaboration in primary care: Barriers and facilitators. International Journal of Integrated Care. 2021;**21**(2):32. DOI: 10.5334/ijic.5589

[12] McInnes S, Peters K, Bonney A, Halcomb E. An integrative review of facilitators and barriers influencing collaboration and teamwork between general practitioners and nurses working in general practice. Journal of Advanced Nursing. 2015;**71**(9):1973-1985. DOI: 10.1111/jan.12647

[13] Schadewaldt V, McInnes E, Hiller JE, Gardner A. Views and experiences of nurse practitioners and medical practitioners with collaborative practice in primary health care – An integrative review.

BMC Family Practice. 2013;**14**(1):132. DOI: 10.1186/1471-2296-14-132

[14] Kuhlmann E, Groenewegen PP, Bond C, Burau V, Hunter DJ. Primary care workforce development in Europe: An overview of health system responses and stakeholder views. Health Policy. 2018;**122**(10):1055-1062

[15] Weller J, Boyd M, Cumin D. Teams, tribes and patient safety: Overcoming barriers to effective teamwork in healthcare. Postgraduate Medical Journal. 2014;**90**(1061):149-154. DOI: 10.1136/postgradmedj-2012-131168

[16] Lemieux-Charles L, McGuire WL. What do we know about health care team effectiveness? A review of the literature. Medical Care Research and Review. 2006;**63**(3):263-300. DOI: 10.1177/1077558706287003

[17] Buljac-Samardzic M, Doekhie KD, van Wijngaarden JDH. Interventions to improve team effectiveness within health care: A systematic review of the past decade. Human Resources for Health. 2020;**18**(1):2. DOI: 10.1186/s12960-019-0411-3

[18] Carter R, Riverin B, Levesque JF, Gariepy G, Quesnel-Vallée A. The impact of primary care reform on health system performance in Canada: A systematic review. BMC Health Services Research. 2016;**16**:324. DOI: 10.1186/s12913-016-1571-7

[19] Cassou M, Mousquès J, Franc C. General practitioners activity patterns: The medium-term impacts of primary care teams in France. Health Policy. 2023;**136**:104868. DOI: 10.1016/j.healthpol.2023.104868

[20] Sinaiko AD, Landrum MB, Meyers DJ, Alidina S, Maeng DD, Friedberg MW, et al. Synthesis of research on patient-centered medical homes brings systematic differences into relief. Health Affairs (Millwood). 2017;**36**(3):500-508. DOI: 10.1377/hlthaff.2016.1235

[21] Strumpf E, Ammi M, Diop M, Fiset-Laniel J, Tousignant P. The impact of team-based primary care on health care services utilization and costs: Quebec's family medicine groups. Journal of Health Economics. 2017;**55**:76-94. DOI: 10.1016/j.jhealeco.2017.06.009

[22] Mickan S, Rodger S. Characteristics of effective teams: A literature review. Australian Health Review. 2000;**23**(3):201-208. DOI: 10.1071/ah000201

[23] Buljac-Samardzic M, Dekker-van Doorn CM, van Wijngaarden JD, van Wijk KP. Interventions to improve team effectiveness: A systematic review. Health Policy. 2010;**94**(3):183-195. DOI: 10.1016/j.healthpol.2009.09.015

[24] Hackman J. The design of work teams. In: Lorsch JW, editor. The Handbook of Organizational Behavior. Englewood Cliffs, NJ: Prentice-Hall; 1987. pp. 315-342

[25] Hackman JR. From causes to conditions in group research. Journal of Organizational Behavior. 2012;**33**(3):428-444. DOI: 10.1002/job.1774

[26] Delalic L, Grøsland M, Gjefsen H. Kontinuitet i Lege-Pasientforholdet. Continuity in Relationship between Doctor and Patient. Oslo: Norwegian Institute of Public Health; 2023

[27] Difi. Innbyggerundersøkelsen 2021. [The Citizen Survey 2021]. Oslo: Difi Direktoratet for forvaltning og ikt; 2021

[28] Pedersen K, Godager G, Tyrihjell J, Værnø S, Gundersen M, Iversen T, et al.

Evaluering av Handlingsplan for Allmennlegetjenesten 2020-2024: Evalueringsrapport II. [Evaluation of the Action Plan for General Practice 2020-2024: Evaluation Report II]. Oslo: Oslo Economics, University of Oslo; 2022

[29] Skyrud K, Rotevatn T. Utvikling i Fastlegenes Arbeidsmengde Og Situasjon over Tid. [Development in General Practitioners' Workload and Situation over Time]. Oslo: Folkehelseinstituttet; 2023

[30] Groenewegen P, Heinemann S, Greß S, Schäfer W. Primary care practice composition in 34 countries. Health Policy. 2015;**119**(12):1576-1583. DOI: 10.1016/j.healthpol.2015.08.005

[31] Helsedirektoratet. Primærhelseteam - Kvalitet, Ledelse Og Finansiering. [Primary Healthcare Team - Quality, Management and Financing]. Oslo: Helsedirektoratet; 2017

[32] Coombs CRH, Cohen T, Duddy C, Mahtani KR, Roberts N, Saini A, et al. Primary care micro-teams: A protocol for an international systematic review to describe and examine the opportunities and challenges of implementation for patients and healthcare professionals. BMJ Open. 2022;**12**(3):e052651. DOI: 10.3399/BJGP.2022.0545

[33] Ghorob A, Bodenheimer T. Building teams in primary care: A practical guide. Families, Systems & Health. 2015;**33**(3):182-192. DOI: 10.1037/fsh0000120

[34] O'Malley AS, Gourevitch R, Draper K, Bond A, Tirodkar MA. Overcoming challenges to teamwork in patient-centered medical homes: A qualitative study. Journal of General Internal Medicine. 2015;**30**(2):183-192. DOI: 10.1007/s11606-014-3065-9

[35] Wagner EH, Flinter M, Hsu C, Cromp D, Austin BT, Etz R, et al. Effective team-based primary care: Observations from innovative practices. BMC Family Practice. 2017;**18**(1):13. DOI: 10.1186/s12875-017-0590-8

[36] Aandahl E, Abelsen B, Fosse A, Godager G, Iversen T, Løyland H, et al. Evaluering Av Pilotprosjekt Med primærhelseteam Og Alternative Finansieringsordninger: Statusrapport V. [Evaluation of a Pilot Project with Primary Healthcare Teams and Alternative Funding Schemes: Status Report no. 5]. Oslo: Oslo Economics, National Centre for Rural Medicine, University of Oslo; 2022

[37] Abelsen B, Gaski M, Godager G, Iversen T, Løyland H, Pedersen K, et al. Evaluering av pilotprosjekt med primærhelseteam og alternative finansieringsordninger: Sluttrapport for 2018-2021 (Statusrapport IV). Oslo: Oslo Economics; 2022

[38] Braun V, Clarke V. Using thematic analysis in psychology. Qualitative Research in Psychology. 2006;**3**(2):77-101. DOI: 10.1191/1478088706qp063oa

[39] Alvesson M, Sköldberg K. Reflexive Methodology: New Vistas for Qualitative Research. 3rd ed. London: Sage; 2018

[40] Li M, Tang H, Liu X. Primary care team and its association with quality of care for people with multimorbidity: A systematic review. BMC Primary Care. 2023;**24**(1):20. DOI: 10.1186/s12875-023-01968-z

[41] Cashman S, Reidy P, Cody K, Lemay C. Developing and measuring progress toward collaborative, integrated, interdisciplinary health care teams. Journal of Interprofessional Care. 2004;**18**(2):183-196. DOI: 10.1080/13561820410001686936

[42] Pullon S, McKinlay E, Dew K. Primary health care in New Zealand: The impact of organisational factors on teamwork. The British Journal of General Practice. 2009;**59**(560):191-197. DOI: 10.3399/bjgp09X395003

[43] Russell GM, Miller WL, Gunn JM, Levesque JF, Harris MF, Hogg WE, et al. Contextual levers for team-based primary care: Lessons from reform interventions in five jurisdictions in three countries. Family Practice. 2018;**35**(3):276-284. DOI: 10.1093/fampra/cmx095

[44] Tuckman B. Developmental sequence in small groups. Psychological Bulletin. 1965;**63**(6):384-399. DOI: 10.1037/h0022100

[45] Donaghy E, Huang H, Henderson D, Wang HH, Guthrie B, Thompson A, et al. Primary care transformation in Scotland: Qualitative evaluation of the views of national senior stakeholders and cluster quality leads. The British Journal of General Practice. 2023;**73**(728):e231-ee41. DOI: 10.3399/BJGP.2022.0186

Chapter 6

How to AID Leadership and Followership in Multidisciplinary Healthcare Teams

Neil E. Grunberg and Erin S. Barry

Abstract

Effective healthcare requires meaningful teamwork among individuals who have diverse knowledge, expertise, experiences, and perspectives. Members of multidisciplinary healthcare teams include many different healthcare professionals—including physicians, nurses, dentists, psychologists, nutritionists, physical therapists, social workers, technicians, researchers, staff, and administrators—as well as patients and their significant others. For multidisciplinary healthcare teams to work effectively and efficiently, it is important to understand teams, members of teams, team processes, relevant principles and practices of leadership and followership, and how to create and maintain high performing teams. This chapter describes each of these concepts; how to assess and develop team members; and how to integrate and apply three particular leadership/followership approaches to optimize or "AID" multidisciplinary healthcare teamwork: adaptive/allostatic, innovative, and distributed/shared/collective leadership and followership. In addition, this chapter discusses how to optimize cohesiveness, morale, performance, and communication of multidisciplinary healthcare teams in the ever-changing contexts in which they work.

Keywords: leadership, followership, adaptive, innovative, distributed, teams, healthcare

1. Introduction

Modern healthcare is a team activity and multidisciplinary teamwork is essential in all healthcare contexts—including preventive medicine and activities to promote health and well-being; at the point of injury/accident and onset of illness; during medical transport; during visits and treatments in clinics, hospitals, and healthcare offices; in home care and hospice; while conducting healthcare research; during healthcare policy and strategic planning; and while administering and conducting healthcare procedures. The traditional, individualist, all-knowing physician working alone and making house calls is a paradigm of the past. Today, optimal healthcare requires input, performance, collaboration, and meaningful teamwork among individuals who have diverse knowledge, expertise, experiences, and perspectives, and who work in multiple settings, both in-person and virtually.

Multidisciplinary teams work across disciplines, generations, professions, and groups to determine how best to provide "STEEP"—safe, timely, effective, efficient, equitable, and patient-centered—care [1]. For multidisciplinary healthcare teams to operate effectively and efficiently, it is important to understand and apply relevant principles and practices of leadership and followership to create and maintain high performing teams.

This chapter first identifies four categories of the many types of multidisciplinary healthcare team members. Next, we discuss what constitutes a team, the two distinctive categories or roles of team members (i.e., as leaders and followers), and team processes. Then, we address how to assess and develop leaders and followers. With this information as a foundation, we describe three leadership and followership approaches that we believe are best suited to "AID" multidisciplinary teams in healthcare settings: adaptive/allostatic; innovative; and distributed/shared/collective. Finally, we present ways to optimize team morale, cohesiveness, performance, including seven strategies for high performing teams and effective communication principles and tips for team members.

1.1 Current members of multidisciplinary healthcare teams

Members of multidisciplinary healthcare teams all contribute to healthcare and well-being. These team members can be categorized into four groups:

a. healthcare professionals and practitioners who deal directly with patients and healthcare activities, including: physicians and nurses with a wide variety of specialties, dentists, psychologists, nutritionists, physical therapists, occupational therapists, social workers, medical equipment and laboratory technicians, case managers, counselors, spiritual advisers, and others

b. healthcare researchers and staff who investigate and identify healthcare best practices and who perform essential operational functions, including: scientists, administrators, fund raisers, operation supervisors, strategic planners, budget and financial analysts, physical plant maintenance workers, purchasing agents, insurance reimbursement staff, policy makers, and others

c. patients and their significant others who are now considered to be members of the healthcare team because it is their care and involvement that is central to mission and because they have ready access to healthcare information via the Internet

d. technology and artificial intelligence (AI) might also be considered as an additional group within multidisciplinary healthcare teams because of contributions to the other three groups' activities.

These groups differ with regard to backgrounds, experiences, education, roles and responsibilities; yet all contribute to and are essential to the well-being of patients and healthcare successes and failures. The challenges for multidisciplinary healthcare teams are: (1) how to work together effectively and efficiently to obtain desired outcomes for patients; (2) to maintain and enhance the well-being of the healthcare team members; and (3) to support the mission and vision of the institutions and systems in which they work. There are opportunities for each individual to contribute

DOI: http://dx.doi.org/10.5772/intechopen.1004644

meaningfully, to experience pride and joy from their contributions, and to receive support and share comradery with colleagues and the healthcare team of which they are members. For multidisciplinary teams to succeed, it is important to understand teams and team processes; the types, roles, and responsibilities of leaders and followers on teams; leadership and followership approaches best suited to multidisciplinary teams in healthcare settings; and how to maximize team performance and well-being. With such a diverse group, it also is critical to know how to optimize communication, cohesiveness, morale, individual and team performance.

1.2 What is a team?

Teams consist of "two or more individuals brought together by an organization or shared mission who are working or interacting on important common goals and are assigned different roles and responsibilities while embedded in an organizational system with linkages to the broader system" ([1], p. 128). More simply, teams are two or more individuals with different roles and responsibilities working together to achieve common goals. Effective teams are: cohesive, have high morale, communicate to achieve mutual understanding, and perform well. Effective teams also reduce errors, improve outcomes, increase job satisfaction, reduce burnout, and use resources effectively [2, 3].

1.3 Members of a team: types and their activities

Teams consist of individuals who are leaders and individuals who are followers (or team members). Leadership and followership refer to activities performed by leaders and followers.

1.3.1 Leaders and leadership relevant to teams

Day [4] defined "leader" as referring to human capital and intrapersonal knowledge, skills, abilities, attitudes, and motivations, whereas "leadership" involves social capital, interpersonal relationships, and organization culture. Of the many definitions offered for each of these words, perhaps the most common single word that describes leaders and leadership is the word "influence" [5–8]. With this emphasis in mind, it is important to recognize that leaders are aspirational and inspirational individuals who influence other individuals, groups, organizations, and systems. Leadership involves the activity of influencing individuals and groups by enhancing behaviors (actions), cognitions (perceptions, thoughts, and beliefs), and motivations (why we act and think as we do) to achieve goals that benefit the individuals and groups [5–8].

Many leader types have been defined, described, and championed as the "best" way to lead. But, in fact, various leader types can be effective depending on the individual leader, team of followers, situation, and context [9, 10]. A partial list of leader types and approaches (in alphabetical order) include: adaptive, affiliative, allostatic, authentic, authoritative, autocratic, change, charismatic, coercive, collective, courageous, cross-cultural, culturally-competent, democratic, distributed, facilitative, heart-centered, innovative, inspirational, laissez-faire, participative, principle-centered, resonant, servant, shared, situational, strategic, thought, transactional, transformational, virtuous, and visionary [7, 10–33].

Each of these leader types and approaches has value and may be well-suited for particular individuals, teams, and situations. However, even a relatively brief description of each of these types of leaders and leadership would require many pages and we believe that is unnecessary to address all of these types and approaches in this chapter about healthcare teams. Instead, we submit that there are three types and approaches that are particularly appropriate and relevant for multidisciplinary teams in healthcare settings:

- Adaptive/allostatic
- Innovative
- Distributed/shared/collective

These three types and approaches "AID" multidisciplinary team success in healthcare settings and are discussed in detail below.

1.3.2 Followers (team members) and followership relevant to teams

In the past, the term follower often has been used to describe individuals who are passive, dependent, or submissive. But this is not how followers are considered today. It is certainly true that leaders usually have more power and authority than do followers. But the importance of leaders is often overestimated, while the importance of followers is often underestimated. Followership refers to the activities of individuals who are not in designated leadership roles.

Followers or "team members" are members of a team who contribute (or not), align (or not) with the leader, and adapt (or not) to the situations and contexts in which they work. Follower types have received much less attention than have leader types. Robert Kelley, Barbara Kellerman, and Ira Chaleff each have written about and described various types of followers. Kelley [34, 35] proposed five follower types classified on two dimensions: dependent-independent thought and passive-active involvement:

- Passive followers do not think for themselves and act passively
- Conformist followers do not think critically, depend on others, and act in accordance with others
- Alienated followers can think for themselves but act passively
- Effective followers are independent thinkers and actively contribute
- Pragmatic survivors adapt to the situation

Kellerman [36] distinguished among five follower types along the dimension of low to high engagement:

- An Isolate is a person who is either physically of psychological assigned to the group, but is not engaged
- A Bystander appears to be physically present and engaged, but does not contribute

- A Participant is probably the most common type of follower and is engaged and contributes to the team's activities
- An Activist is engaged and also initiates conversations, offers ideas and perspectives, and suggests alternative approaches for the team to achieve its goals
- A Diehard is a do or die extremist; it's their way or no way at all

Chaleff [37, 38] focused on whether followers have the courage to either support or to oppose the leader and identified seven ways followers can either be courageous or not:

- Assuming responsibility for self, team, and organization
- Serving the leader
- Challenging others about what is ethically and morally right
- Participating in transformation if change is needed
- Taking moral action if they decide to oppose the leader
- Speaking to the hierarchy about the organization
- Convincing leaders to listen to followers in support of courageous followership

Barry and Grunberg [39] built upon all three of these models of follower types by: using a dimension of engagement based on Kellerman and similar to Kelley's activity dimension; adding an orthogonal dimension ranging from aligned or not aligned with the leader and/or team; and indicating that followers may or may not have the courage (per Chaleff) to align or not align with the leader. According to this integrated model of follower types (see **Figure 1**):

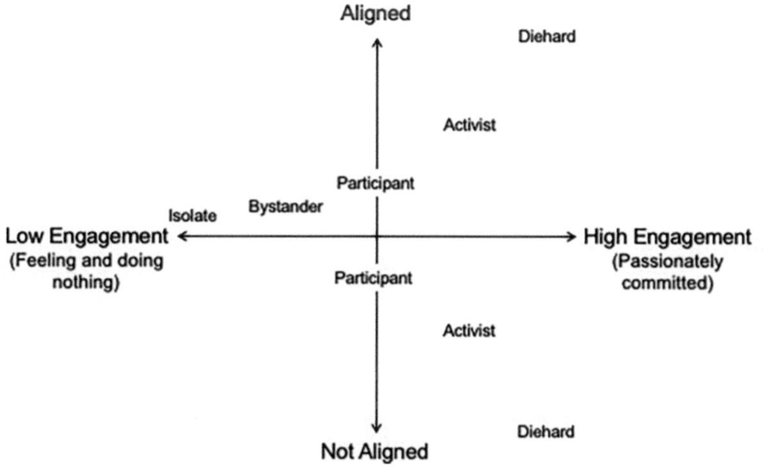

Figure 1.
Follower styles along the axes of engagement and alignment.

- An Isolate is neither aligned or not aligned with the leader and/or team
- A Bystander may appear to be aligned with the leader and/or team, but their lack of engagement leaves them essentially neutral with regard to alignment
- A Participant can either align with the leader and/or team or cannot align, possibly depending on and in accordance with the alignment of the other followers
- An Activist can align with the leader and/or team and contribute in ways to support the leader and/or team or cannot align and contribute in ways that oppose the leader and/or team
- A Diehard is the most extreme type of follower and either aligns 100% with the leader and/or team or opposes the leader and/or team 100%

In **Figure 1**, notice that the position of the five types is not linear on the alignment dimension, but exponential as once followers start engaging, there is more evidence of alignment or no alignment with the leader and/or team.

It also is noteworthy that follower type, with regard to engagement and alignment, might vary (or adapt) depending on situations and context where context includes urgency of mission/goal, time, resources, leader and leadership types and approaches, and relationships among team members. It is also important to note that being "not aligned" is sometimes the best approach. For example, if the leader is taking the group in an inappropriate direction, then followers should have the courage to not align. Or, if the demands required to align with the leader are unreasonable or impossible, then the followers should have the courage to not align.

Each of these follower types has value and may be well-suited for particular individuals, teams, and situations. However, as indicated above regarding leader types, we submit that the three types of leader/leadership that we advocate as particularly appropriate and relevant for multidisciplinary teams in healthcare settings, also should be applied to followers/followership on multidisciplinary teams in healthcare settings:

- Adaptive/allostatic
- Innovative
- Distributed/shared/collective

These three types of leadership/followership that AID team success are discussed in more detail below.

1.4 Team processes

Leaders and followers can interact effectively in different ways. According to Richard Hackman [40], the roles and responsibilities of leaders and team members (i.e., followers) can vary, but that it is important for all members to understand their roles and responsibilities and the team process that is operating (see **Figure 2**). Specifically, in:

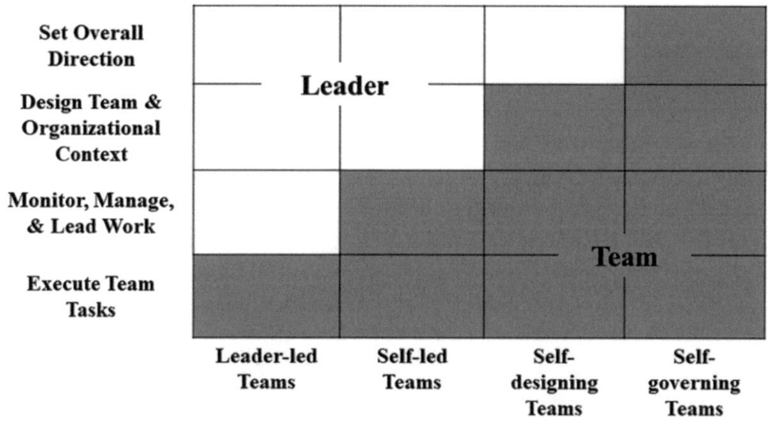

Figure 2.
Team processes based on Hackman [40].

- Leader-led teams, the leader sets the overall direction, designs the team and organizational context, monitors and manages the work of the team, while team members perform the team tasks

- Self-managing teams, the leader sets the overall direction and designs the team and organizational context, while the team members monitor, manage, and perform the work

- Self-designing teams, the leader sets the overall direction, while the team members design the team and organizational context, monitor, manage, and perform the work

- Self-governing teams, team members set the overall direction, design the team and organizational context, monitor and manage the work, and perform the tasks

As mentioned above, it is important to think about leadership and followership as activities and not as static positions [41, 42]. Based on this principle, anyone can lead and anyone can follow, from any position, anytime, anywhere. One person may lead the group in particular situations or through specific tasks while other team members follow; and other team members (who are usually followers) may either lead when they have knowledge, skills, or perspectives to share that will optimize team performance and goal attainment. To lead, you must take ownership of what you are doing and engage others to get them engaged to achieve mission and common goals.

1.5 Team processes in healthcare settings

The particular team process best suited to multidisciplinary teams in healthcare settings depends on several factors, including: knowledge, experience, skills of the team members (including leader and followers); the healthcare setting and conditions; resources available; time and urgency of decision-making and actions; potential outcomes and consequences of actions. For example, the best team process in a busy Emergency Room with an unstable patient, where decisions and actions must be made quickly differs from the best team process in a discussion of a complex, multifaceted medical case for which the patient is stable. The best team process in a field setting (e.g., at the site of a traffic accident, military conflict under fire, or humanitarian relief effort to a natural disaster) differs from the best team process during a strategic planning session among hospital financial analysts and administrators discussing what healthcare specialties or services to add or to cut and what real estate to purchase. The best team process for laboratory bench scientists studying biopsychosocial mechanisms underlying a particular disease differs from the best team process for researchers and staff conducting community outreach and gathering survey data. The best team process used by a team of experienced members who have worked together successfully for years differs from a team led by an experienced individual and staffed by novice followers. It is important for all members of a team to understand their roles and responsibilities, team process options, and which team process is being applied and why in order to optimize buy-in and meaningful participation from all members and to minimize interpersonal conflict that often results from misunderstandings or poor communication. It also is important for teams to regularly reevaluate the team process that is in effect to determine if the process should be changed as the team members and situation change.

2. How to assess and develop leaders and followers (including oneself and others): the leader-follower framework (LF2)

Regardless of individual leader and follower types as well as the team process best suited to each multidisciplinary team and each healthcare setting, it is essential to be able to assess and develop ourselves and other team members as leaders and as followers as well as assess and develop as a team. One conceptual framework for assessment and development is the Leader-Follower Framework (LF2) [5, 6] that was developed through a comprehensive review of the relevant, extant, scholarly, and historical literatures and the leader development approaches used by the U.S. Army, Navy, Air Force, Coast Guard, and Public Health Service. The LF2 includes four "C" elements—Character, Competence, Context, Communication—that are applied and interact across four psychosocial levels—Personal, Interpersonal, Team, and Organizational. We believe the LF2 provides a valuable way to assess and develop all members of teams. Each element of the LF2 is briefly explained below.

Character (Who we are) includes physical and psychological aspects of each individual. Character includes physical demographics and appearance, personality, attitudes, beliefs, and values. To know and understand our own Character requires internal self-awareness. To know and understand how others perceive and react to us requires external self-awareness. Effective leaders and followers work to develop Character in positive ways, adapting to situations, changing to meet new situations optimally, and adjusting to team processes and to other team members to optimize team morale, cohesiveness, and performance.

Competence (What we know and do) refers to the knowledge and skills relevant to perform a particular role (e.g., health care professionals, practitioners, scientists, administrators, support staff, patients, significant others). Competence also includes the broader knowledge and skills that transcend those particular roles (e.g., critical thinking, decision-making, problem solving, motivating others, conflict resolution, emotional intelligence). Effective leaders and followers work to develop Competence in themselves and others to optimize team morale, cohesiveness, and performance.

Context (When and Where we act) includes physical states outside of us (e.g., day/night; hot/cold; urban/rural), physical states within us (e.g., full/poorly nourished; rested/tired; healthy/unhealthy), our psychological condition (e.g., calm, anxious, depressed), social group and team (e.g., number of people, relationships among the individuals), and cultural (e.g., lived experiences, cultural norms, values, belief systems) environments. Context also includes effects of stress (physical and psychological) that can alter well-being, individual and team interactions, and performance. Demands and consequences of healthcare activities and outcomes are often extremely stressful and must be addressed and mitigated to avoid deleterious effects on individuals and teams, including burnout and medical errors.

Communication (How we exchange information) includes both sending and receiving information, verbally and nonverbally. Verbal communication can be transmitted in writing or orally. Nonverbal communication includes body language, spatial distance, facial expressions, and paralanguage (e.g., volume, tone, phrasing, speed). Verbal and nonverbal communication must be clear, respectful, and consistent to optimize team performance. Sending and receiving communication skills are relevant to communicate critical information and to achieve mutual understanding. Clear, understandable, and accurate information is of the utmost importance among all members of multidisciplinary teams in healthcare settings. Communication is so important to team success that Principles and Elements of Communication are presented in more detail later in this chapter.

Personal refers to each individual. Interpersonal refers to dyadic relationships and interactions among any two people, including leader with follower, team member with another team member. Team refers to all of the members (leader and followers) of the group of people who are mutually committed to common goals. Organizational refers to large groups, institutions, and systems.

3. Leadership and followership approaches for multidisciplinary teams in healthcare settings

As discussed above, there are many different types and approaches relevant to leadership and followership. The best approach depends on the individual people involved as well as the situation and resources available. However, we believe that there are three approaches that are especially relevant to multidisciplinary teams to optimize performance, mission accomplishment, and well-being of team members. We offer the acronym "AID" to help remember that the application and integration of these three approaches—adaptive/allostatic, innovative, distributed/shared/collective—will help multidisciplinary teams succeed in healthcare settings. Each of these three approaches is described below.

3.1 Adaptive/allostatic leadership and followership

Heifetz et al. [16] described "adaptive" leaders as those who use their skills and insights to respond and adapt to challenging situations; manage themselves depending on environmental demands; and help team members tolerate and respond to challenging conditions. Adaptive leaders respond effectively to variable, uncertain, complex, and ambiguous (VUCA) environments. As such, this approach is well-suited to the challenges, demands, and opportunities of healthcare situations and settings to perform effectively and to avoid burnout.

Yarnell and Grunberg [23] built upon Heifetz and colleagues' notion by advocating for "allostatic" leaders and leadership—adaptation that includes learning, changing, and strengthening following each experience. These ideas can, and should, be considered within followers and followership as well. The process of allostasis refers to adaptive processes that involve "achieving stability through change" [43]. This type of adaptation is in response to a given situation or challenge and often results in a post-challenge strengthening. Allostatic individuals, therefore, adapt to, learn from, and change in response to experiences and challenges in ways that improve their abilities to respond effectively to future challenges and to minimize negative responses and burnout. Using a physiological analogy, increases in heart rate and blood pressure to physical or psychological stressor are adaptive and return to baseline values post-stress. In contrast, immunological responses to infections are allostatic as they adapt to the infections and are changed and strengthened post-infection to be prepared to better respond to future, similar infections. Similarly, adaptive individuals respond to challenge, whereas allostatic individuals adapt and change in response to a challenge. Both adaptive and allostatic approaches are valuable for all members of multidisciplinary teams in healthcare settings where adapting to challenge is necessary. Additionally, the strengthening post-challenge is valuable to maintain physical and psychological well-being to be well-prepared for subsequent situations and challenges.

3.2 Innovative Leadership and followership

Innovative leadership and followership emphasize acceptance of (or "structured") change within oneself; the team members; and the skills, knowledge, and tools relevant to each situation. Innovative leadership and followership seek to maximize engagement, cohesiveness, and performance of the team. Innovative individuals constantly develop and grow by learning new, relevant approaches and unlearning old, outdated approaches. This approach also requires understanding, inspiring, and engaging followers/followership to change appropriately in order to achieve team successes, cohesiveness, and morale. Innovative leadership and followership are especially relevant to healthcare settings today because of the rapid and profound changes in knowledge and best practices, as well as current advances in technology and Artificial Intelligence relevant to healthcare issues. In fact, Metcalf et al. [44] recently addressed these issues in *Innovative Leadership and Followership in the Age of AI: A Guide to Creating Your Future as Leader, Follower, and AI Ally*. The Innovative approach encourages innovative individuals to exercise:

- Strategic activities—inspiring team members and setting organization vision and culture

- Tactical activities—influencing team members' actions and organization systems and processes

- Holistic activities—aligning team members with their organization

- Self-awareness—consisting of internal self-awareness (i.e., awareness of our values, personality, style, strengths, biases, and so on) and external self-awareness (how others perceive our values, personality, style, strengths, biases, etc.)

DOI: http://dx.doi.org/10.5772/intechopen.1004644

In addition, it is relevant to consider and develop the seven elements central to the Innovative Leadership Framework. These elements are categorized either with regard to Individual Development (for oneself and others) or Organizational Development:

Elements of Individual Development

- Leader type refers to core predispositions, traits, and attitudes
- Developmental perspective is how to make sense of experiences
- Mindset includes beliefs, attitudes, and assumptions that guide thoughts and actions
- Resilience is the ability to adapt to change
- Skills and behaviors are specific abilities and actions

Elements of Organizational Development

- Organizational context and situational analysis involve understanding interactions with teams and organizations
- Lead followers and organization to optimize wellness and performance of team members

3.3 Distributed/shared/collective leadership and followership

In addition to applying leadership and followership approaches to multidisciplinary health settings that emphasize Adapting and Innovating, it also is essential for the members of healthcare teams to understand and embrace approaches that allow and encourage those team members (i.e., designated leaders and followers) who have the most relevant knowledge, skills, perspectives to perform leadership activities. There are three related, but distinct, approaches to achieve this type of team activity: distributed, shared, and collective leadership and followership. Each of these approaches is of value to teams in healthcare settings. Which of these related approaches is optimal, depends on the members of the team, situation, and the context.

3.3.1 Distributed Leadership and followership

Distributed leadership and followership focus on distributing the leadership and followership roles, tasks, and decision-making authority across various individuals or teams within an organization depending on the situation and context. This approach often involves different units or departments within an organization, where leadership responsibilities are divided based upon knowledge, skills, and specializations enabling a flexible, adaptive structure. Distributed leadership and followership emphasize interactions among units and team members [24–26].

3.3.2 Shared leadership and followership

Shared leadership and followership emphasize the active participation and collaboration among all members of the team who, as a whole, collectively influence and guide the group's decisions and activities. The key to shared leadership and followership is the influence of the group versus the influence of one or a few members of the group. This approach usually occurs within a specific small team, where team members collaborate and share leadership and followership responsibilities based on their differences in expertise. Shared leadership and followership involve all team members contributing to the team's performance in service of mission and goals where every team member assumes responsibility for their contributions to the team and mission [27–30].

3.3.3 Collective leadership and followership

Collective leadership and followership emphasize collaboration and equal participation among all members, regardless of each individual's roles or positions. The focus is on leveraging diverse perspectives and fostering a sense of shared ownership. This approach is more holistic and encompasses the entire organization or community—everyone is encouraged to contribute their own unique insights, perspectives, knowledge, and skills to achieve the common goal. This approach maximizes inclusive and democratic decision-making process [30–33]. Collective leadership and followership emphasize consensus building and, where necessary, conflict resolution regarding team-relevant decisions requiring mutual trust, effective communication, and shared learning among team members as roles and responsibilities shift [45]. Collective leadership and followership emphasize transformation, participation, collaboration, and commitment [46].

4. How to optimize team morale, cohesiveness, performance

Understanding leaders/leadership, followers/followership, team process options, and leadership and followership approaches will help to optimize multidisciplinary team cohesiveness, morale, and performance in healthcare settings. It is important to be aware of and to apply strategies that are central to high performing teams. In addition, it is useful to be aware of characteristics of effective versus dysfunctional teams.

4.1 Seven strategies for high performing teams

There are seven strategies to optimize performance of teams.

4.1.1 Vision

Creating a clear vision, sense of purpose, and goal(s) for the team is extremely important and is built on communication. Without a clear vision or sense of purpose, teams will struggle to know what to do, to feel valued, and to want to complete the work [47]. When everyone knows the end state, the team members can work collaboratively towards the goal and hold each other accountable. This communication allows leadership to let everyone know where the team is heading, but they do not need to provide every detail about how the team will get there. Interestingly, the best way to lead a team is when the leader specifies the ends (i.e., goals) but does not tell the team members exactly how to achieve the goal (i.e., the means) [40]. This strategy enables team members to offer their own ideas, approaches, and skills to achieve the team goal, allowing each team member to maximize contributions and feel valued and part of the team. In many cases, leaders assume that they need to specify both the ends and the means, yet this approach often leads to wasted human resources because it does not allow or encourage team members to offer their own ideas or maximally contribute their knowledge and skills to the work. When neither the ends or the means are specified, the result is likely anarchy—team members do not know the goal they are working towards and they do they know how to work towards that unknown goal. When ends are not specified, but the means are specified, team members have no idea what they are working towards, but they are being micromanaged and told exactly what to do, which may lead to apathy and burn out.

4.1.2 Clarity around roles

All team members need to have clarity around roles. They need to understand their own roles and responsibilities as well as the roles and responsibilities of the other team members. Without this information, individuals may unknowingly complete the same tasks, which could lead to conflict, misunderstandings, and wasted time and resources. When roles are known to all members of the team, they are able to complete their parts and also step in to help others when needed. It also allows for teams to work collectively towards the common goal and can improve decision making, action plans, and commitment to the team [47–49].

4.1.3 Respect

Teams that have mutual respect and appreciate all team members—leaders and followers—are highly effectively. Each member of the team recognizes that each individual has valuable skills and experiences to bring to the team. This perspective allows all team members to value each other and to feel valued as members of the team [47].

4.1.4 Flexibility

Flexibility is essential from all team members to allow them to adapt to on-going changes within the team and the context in which they work. In many cases, healthcare teams work in physically and emotionally challenging environments that may constantly change [50] and team members need to be aware of the context and how it is relevant to team performance [47, 48].

4.1.5 Safety

It is also important to create a psychologically safe environment for all members of a team to allow for transfer of ideas, conflict management, and movement between leader and follower roles [47, 51, 52]. Every team member should be able to speak up and to contribute to the team, including input that criticizes some aspect of the current team or identifies an emerging problem. In a psychologically safe space, all team members can offer ways to improve the team's functioning, even if that means speaking up against the direction set by the leader or by other team members. For teams to operate with psychological safety, it is particularly important for members to [53]:

- Demonstrate engagement (e.g., being present and focusing on the conversation)

- Show understanding (e.g., summarize input from others and indicate understanding)
- Be inclusive in interpersonal settings (e.g., express gratitude for input from others)
- Be inclusive in decision making (e.g., solicit input from others)
- Show confidence and conviction without appearing to be inflexible (e.g., manage effectively)

4.1.6 Manage conflict

It is important for individuals to effectively manage conflict that occurs on the team and to be aware how each team members perceives conflict. Many people have a negative perception of conflict, whereas others perceive conflict as opportunities to understand others' viewpoints. How individuals deal with team conflict can impact team effectiveness. Adam Grant [54] distinguishes between relationship conflict and task conflict. Relationship conflict refers to personal, emotional clashes that include friction and animosity, and task conflict refers to clashes about ideas and opinions. In his research Grant found that poor performing teams focus more on relationship conflicts. High performing teams minimize relationship conflict and, instead, focus on task conflict to emphasize finding the best path forward rather than personal feelings.

4.1.7 Celebrate achievement

Individual and team achievements should be clearly valued and celebrated. When team members feel valued and respected, they will want to perform to the best of their ability to support the team. Feeling valued can build trust and cohesion and a supportive environment where teams can more effectively adapt when challenges arise.

5. Communication principles and elements to optimize team performance

As discussed above, Communication is the "how" of leadership and followership. Effective communication is critical for multidisciplinary teams in healthcare settings because whether communication is clear and understood or unclear and misunderstood can be the difference between sound healthcare versus medical errors, well-being versus injury/illness, life versus death. Effective communication also is central to establishing and building high performing teams. Therefore, we address principles and elements of communication in more detail here. The principles listed below are based on the extant psychology literature regarding persuasive communication. The elements listed below are how to best structure communication.

5.1 Principles to optimize effective communication among team members

- *Authenticity* is best conveyed when you have high self-awareness of your values, attitudes, beliefs, biases, and genuinely express your views, interest in others, commitment to your role and responsibilities, and awareness of how you are perceived by others

- *Clarity* refers to whether information is understandable to the receiver of communications

- *Cognitive heuristics and biases* refer to ways of perceiving and thinking that affect whether we believe, understand, remember particular information, and make decisions

- *Consistency of verbal and non-verbal communication* is important to strengthen and reinforce a given communication

- *Perceived credibility* refers to the credentials, expertise, or standing of an individual relevant to information conveyed and influences the impact of the communication

- *Perceived self-interest* refers to whether the communicator has a real or perceived vested interest or personal interest in the information conveyed which can undermine or weaken their credibility

- *Point/counterpoint* refers to presentation of alternatives with support and opposition to the alternatives that are presented

- *Primacy* refers to the fact that people tend to focus on and remember information that they first receive and first impressions

- *Recency* refers to the fact that people also focus on and remember the most recent information they receive, including "take-home" messages

- *Repetition* refers to the fact that people focus on, believe, and remember information that is repeated

- *"Sleeper" effect* refers to the phenomenon that people tend to forget the source of information while remembering content or emotion associated with a communication. Therefore, the power of information has the greatest long-lasting effect

5.2 Elements of communication relevant to effective communication

- *Be present* because effective communication requires senders and receivers to convey that they are genuinely interested in others

- *Body language*, including hand gestures, touching, distance, can affirm or detract from effective communication and should be consistent with content and intent

- *Facial expressions* can be as or even more powerful and informative than words, so they must be consistent with words and communication intent

- *Humor* can be a powerful part of communication, but senders must be sensitive to receivers' reactions, especially when conveying serious information common in healthcare settings

- *Phrasing* of oral words within communications affects understanding (e.g., grouping subjects, predicates, asides, series, and other elements of sentences)

- *Pitch and intonation* in oral communications convey emotion and should be consistent with content and intent

- *Rhythm* in speech conveys emotion, can come across as more relaxed versus more serious and, therefore, should be adjusted depending on content and intent of communication

- *Silence* is important at appropriate points in communication for information to be processed, exchanged, and understood

- *Tempo* is the speed of delivery and depends on individual differences, culture, age, and state of arousal, and should be adjusted to maximize understanding

- *Tone* of voice conveys emotions and should be consistent with content and intent of communications

- *Verbal tics* refer to the unintentional sounds or words that add "noise" to communications and should be avoided. They include: um, ah, you know, sort of, kind of, I mean, right

- *Vocabulary, phrases, jargon, grammar, syntax* includes words and phrases that accurately represent the information intended to be conveyed and should be understandable to receivers of communications

- *Volume* is how loud or soft the sender communicates verbal information and must consider setting, ambient sound, receivers hearing, and intent of communication

6. Summary and conclusions

Effective multidisciplinary teamwork in healthcare settings is essential to maximize team success and well-being. Members of multidisciplinary healthcare teams include: healthcare professionals and practitioners, healthcare researchers and staff, patients and their significant others; technology and Artificial Intelligence. To create and maintain effective multidisciplinary teams in healthcare settings, it is important to understand: types and activities of team members (including leaders and followers); team processes; how to assess and develop team members. It also is important to understand leadership and followership approaches, especially three approaches that can "AID" multidisciplinary healthcare teams: adaptive/allostatic; innovative; distributed/shared/collective. In addition, to optimize team cohesiveness, morale, and performance, it is important to practice high-performing team strategies and to communicate effectively.

Acknowledgements

Disclaimer: The opinions and assertions contained herein are the sole ones of the authors and are not to be construed as reflecting the views of the Uniformed Services University or the Department of Defense of the United States of America.

Conflict of interest

The authors declare no conflicts of interest.

Author details

Neil E. Grunberg* and Erin S. Barry
Uniformed Services University, Bethesda, Maryland, USA

*Address all correspondence to: neil.grunberg@usuhs.edu

References

[1] Higginson J, Hofler L, Hammoud MM. Principles of teamwork and team science. In: Skochelak SE, Hammoud MM, Lomis KD, Borkan JM, Gonzalo JD, Lawson LE, Starr SR, editors. Health Systems Science. Philadelphia, PA: Elsevier; 2021. pp. 127-138

[2] Rosen MA et al. Teamwork in healthcare: Key discoveries enabling safer, high-quality care. American Psychologist. 2018;**73**(4):433

[3] Bisbey TM et al. Teams of psychologists helping teams: The evolution of the science of team training. American Psychologist. 2019;**74**(3):278

[4] Day DV. Leadership development: A review in context. The Leadership Quarterly. 2001;**11**(4):581-613

[5] Barry ES, Grunberg NE. A conceptual framework to guide leader and follower education, development, and assessment. Journal of Leadership, Accountability, and Ethics. 2020;**17**(1):127-134

[6] Callahan CW, Grunberg NE. Military medical leadership. In: O'Connor FG, Schoomaker EB, Smith DC, editors. Fundamentals of Military Medicine. San Antonio, TX: Borden Institute; 2019. pp. 51-66

[7] Northouse PG. Leadership: Theory and Practice. 8th ed. Los Angeles, CA: Sage Publications; 2018

[8] Yukl G. Leadership in Organizations. Upper Saddle River, NJ: Pearson Education; 1981

[9] Day DV, The nature of leadership development. In: Day DV, Antonakis J, editors. The Nature of Leadership. Thousand Oaks, CA: Sage Publications; 2012

[10] Goethals G, Sorenson G, Burns J. Encyclopedia of Leadership. Thousand Oaks, CA: Sage Publications; 2004

[11] Bean-Mellinger B. Six Leadership Styles. 2017. Available from: http://smallbusiness.chron.com/six-leadership-styles-54300.html

[12] Blanken R. 8 Common Leadership Styles. 2017. Available from: https://www.asaecenter.org/resources/articles/an_magazine/2013/january/8-common-leadership-styles

[13] Boyatzis R, McKee A. Resonant Leadership: Renewing Yourself and Connecting with Others Through Mindfulness, Hope, and Compassion. Boston, MA: Harvard Business School Press; 2005

[14] Covey SR. Principle-Centred Leadership. New York, NY: Simon and Schuster; 1991

[15] Day DV, Antonakis J, The Nature of Leadership. In: Day DV, Antonakis J, editors. Thousand Oaks. CA Sage: Publications; 2012

[16] Heifetz RA, Linsky M, Grashow A. The Practice of Adaptive Leadership: Tools and Tactics for Changing Your Organization and the World. Cambridge, MA: Harvard Business Press; 2009

[17] Johnson, R. 5 Different Types of Leadership Styles. 2017. Available from: http://smallbusiness.chron.com/5-different-types-leadership-styles-17584.html

[18] Kilburg RR. Virtuous Leaders: Strategy, Character, and Influence in the 21st Century. Washington, DC: American Psychological Association; 2012

[19] Lewin K, Lippit R, White RK. Patterns of aggressive behavior in experimentally created social climates. Journal of Social Psychology. 1939;**10**:271-301

[20] Raza, A. 12 Different Types of Leadership Styles. 2017. Available from: http://wisetoast.com/12-different-types-of-leadership-styles/

[21] Thornton PB. 2013. Four Types of Leaders: All Leaders Want to Change the Status Quo, but they Use Different Means. Available from: https://trainingmag.com/four-types-leaders

[22] Crowe RP et al. Defining components of team leadership and membership in prehospital emergency medical services. Prehospital Emergency Care. 2017;**21**(5):645-651

[23] Yarnell A, Grunberg NE. Developing "allostatic leaders": A psychobiosocial perspective. In: Clark M, Gruber C, editors. Leader Development Deconstructed. Cham, Switzerland: Springer International Publishing; 2017. pp. 23-50

[24] Whitby GB. Distributive leadership as an emerging concept. Australian Centre for Educational Leadership. 2006;**22**(2):08

[25] Woods PA et al. Variabilities and dualities in distributed leadership: Findings from a systematic literature review. Educational Management Administration & Leadership. 2004;**32**(4):439-457

[26] Beirne M. The reforming appeal of distributed leadership. British Journal of Healthcare Management. 2017;**23**(6):262-270

[27] Zhu J et al. Shared leadership: A state-of-the-art review and future research agenda. Journal of Organizational Behavior. 2018;**39**(7):834-852

[28] Carson JB, Tesluk PE, Marrone JA. Shared leadership in teams: An investigation of antecedent conditions and performance. Academy of Management Journal. 2007;**50**(5):1217-1234

[29] Janssens S et al. Shared leadership in healthcare action teams: A systematic review. Journal of Patient Safety. 2021;**17**(8):e1441-e1451

[30] Yammarino FJ et al. Collectivistic leadership approaches: Putting the "we" in leadership science and practice. Industrial and Organizational Psychology. 2012;**5**(4):382-402

[31] Contractor NS et al. The topology of collective leadership. The Leadership Quarterly. 2012;**23**(6):994-1011

[32] Friedrich TL, Griffith JA, Mumford MD. Collective leadership behaviors: Evaluating the leader, team network, and problem situation characteristics that influence their use. The Leadership Quarterly. 2016;**27**(2):312-333

[33] Mumford MD et al. Collective leadership: Thinking about issues vis-à-vis others. Industrial and Organizational Psychology. 2012;**5**(4):408-411

[34] Kelley RE. Rethinking followership. In: Riggio RE, Chaleff I, Lipman-Blumen J, editors. The Art of Followership: How Great Followers Create Great Leaders and Organizations. San Francisco, CA: Jossey-Bass; 2008. pp. 5-16

[35] Kelley RE. In praise of followers. Harvard Business Review. 1988;**66**:142-148

[36] Kellerman B. Followership: How Followers Are Creating Change and Changing Leaders. Boston, MA: Harvard Business School Press Boston; 2008

[37] Chaleff I. The Courageous Follower: Standing uSp to & for Our Leaders. Berrett-Koehler Publishers; 2009

[38] Chaleff I. The Courageous Follower. San Francisco, CA: Berrett-Koehler Publishers; 1995

[39] Barry ES, Grunberg NE. Healthcare teams. In: Quinn JF, White BA, editors. Cultivating Leadership in Medicine. Dubuque, IA: Kendall Hunt Publishing Company; 2019. pp. 117-130

[40] Hackman JR. Leading Teams: Setting the Stage for Great Performances. Boston, MA: Harvard Business School Publishing Corporation; 2002

[41] Green C, McBride JF. Teaching Leadership: Case-in Point, Case Studies and Coaching. Wichita, KS: KLC Press; 2015

[42] O'Malley E, McBride JF. When Everyone Leads the Toughest Challenges Get Seen and Solved. Portland, OR: Bard Press; 2023

[43] Sterling P, Eyer J. Allostasis: A new paradigm to explain arousal pathology. In: Fisher S, Reason JT, editors. Handbook of Life Stress, Cognition, and Health. Chicester, NY: Wiley; 1988

[44] Metcalf M et al. Leadership and Followership in the Age of AI: A Guide to Creating Your Future as Leader, Follower, and AI Ally. Phronesis Publishing; 2023

[45] Shonk K. What Is Collective Leadership. Daily Blog: Program of Negotiation Harvard Law School; 2023

[46] Collar M. 2013. Available from: https://www.shrm.org/hr-today/news/hr-news/pages/spring-2013-collective-leadership.aspx

[47] Barry ES et al. Leadership and followership in military interprofessional healthcare teams. Military Medicine. 2021;**186**(S3):7-15

[48] Varpio L et al. Interprofessional healthcare teams in the military: A scoping literature review. Military Medicine. 2018;**183**(11/12):e448-e454

[49] Bell ST et al. Team composition and the ABCs of teamwork. American Psychologist. 2018;**73**(4):349

[50] Ervin JN et al. Teamwork in the intensive care unit. American Psychologist. 2018;**73**(4):468

[51] Edmondson AC et al. Understanding psychological safety in health care and education organizations: A comparative perspective. Research in Human Development. 2016;**13**(1):65-83

[52] O'Donovan R, McAuliffe E. Exploring psychological safety in healthcare teams to inform the development of interventions: Combining observational, survey and interview data. BMC Health Services Research. 2020;**20**(1):1-16

[53] Edmondson AC. The Fearless Organization: Creating Psychological Safety in the Workplace for Learning, Innovation, and Growth. Hoboken, NJ: John Wiley & Sons; 2018

[54] Grant A. Think Again: The Power of Knowing What You Don't Know. New York, NY: Penguin; 2021

Chapter 7

Perspective Chapter: Opportunities and Barriers to Effective Multidisciplinary Teamwork in the Education and Training of Allied-Healthcare Students

Kirpa Chandan, Russell Hitchen and Rupal Lovell-Patel

Abstract

Collaboration between different allied-healthcare professionals through multi-disciplinary teamwork can help lead to integrated care and subsequently better outcomes for patients. Based on their experiences, the authors reflect upon both the advantages and the challenges to effective teamwork in a healthcare setting. They consider how higher education and training of allied-healthcare students could benefit from greater cross-professional collaboration, and they give their perspectives on the barriers and constraints to collaboration across disciplines. Within this chapter, the three authors who are all both university educators and allied-healthcare professionals, also deliberate on a specific example of head injury/concussion where there is potential opportunity to improve collaboration across their respective professions of Audiology, Physiotherapy and Optometry. They explore how cross-professional collaboration may help to provide improved patient-centred care.

Keywords: multi-disciplinary teamwork (MDT), patient-centred care, collaboration, allied healthcare, head injury/concussion

1. Introduction

This chapter considers both the opportunities and barriers to employing multi-disciplinary approaches in both healthcare settings and in the training of allied healthcare students. The authors' experiences of multi-disciplinary approaches in healthcare and cross-professional collaboration in education will be examined. They discuss some examples within their own specialisms of cross collaboration in the academic setting. This discussion is set in the context of the continued importance of allied healthcare professionals providing individualised patient-centred care.

2. Multi-disciplinary approaches within healthcare settings

The World-Health Organisation (WHO) [1] states that current health services are not sufficient for 21st century challenges and that half the world's population does not have access to essential health care. It is evident that even in developed first world countries, healthcare settings are posing ever more challenging for medical, nursing and allied-healthcare professionals for multiple contributing reasons including but not limited to: the ageing population; increases in waiting lists for assessments, diagnoses, and interventions/treatments; shortage of resources; difficulties recruiting staff and difficulties retaining staff; sometimes ineffective training pathways for some professions; lack of funding and variation in referral pathways. Therefore, it is particularly important to continue to develop more effective and streamlined processes and procedures in healthcare. There is a gradual move towards increasing holistic and multidisciplinary approaches in healthcare [2].

A multidisciplinary team (MDT) is defined by the United Kingdom's (UK) National Health Service (NHS) as a group of health and care staff from different organisations and professions that work together to make decisions regarding the treatment of individual patients and users [3]. Typically, patients want efficient organised healthcare suited to their needs [4]. The main driving force in introducing multi-disciplinary approaches in healthcare is to help to provide patient-centred care [4]. Such multi-disciplinary approaches in healthcare settings are becoming increasingly more important because they can also potentially help with ever increasing cost and waiting list challenges. Additionally, for more complex pathologies, one may argue that a multi-disciplinary approach is the most efficient and useful way to manage such patients [5]. A MDT can come together to achieve a common goal for patients with complex pathologies [5].

3. Multi-disciplinary approaches within higher education

Traditionally, students studying healthcare programmes were educated in "silos" throughout their studies [6]. Yet when they graduated, they were expected to function as part of a wider MDT where they would have to collaborate with other medical, nursing and healthcare professionals [6].

As a result of ever expanding scientific, technological, research, and other discoveries, there needs to be a reflection on the entire professional training curriculum [2]. It is important that future generations of healthcare professionals are encouraged to engage in MDT working from early on in their studies. Many allied healthcare professional subjects/specialisms are taught at tertiary, higher education level. Amongst these different subjects, there is considerable variation in the level of cross subject and/or multi-disciplinary learning and teaching. Often, it is the case that the level of collaboration is limited in the respect that it is typically more generic topics such as research methods, professional skills, clinical governance, and so forth that may be taught to multiple groups of students across multiple disciplines at once. It is often the case, that the subject specific items are taught by the subject specialists to students in that particular subject area. In many cases, students are taught within the confines of a discipline-specific curriculum and students studying these programmes have little exposure to working with other disciplines [6]. Over time, there has been a shift to try and provide more interactive learning between and amongst individuals from various health professions [6]. Yet, there is potential scope for much more collaboration amongst teaching professionals across multiple subject areas. This increased collaboration amongst teaching professionals could potentially enhance the learning experience for the learners. An example of this type of first-hand reflection on collaboration in healthcare education is the current first author whose specialism is Audiology being invited by the second author whose specialisms is Physiotherapy, to deliver lectures on head injury and the audio-vestibular system to a group of Physiotherapy and Sports Medicine students. Other allied healthcare professionals such as Optometrists and Dentists were also invited to deliver topics on head injury and the effects on the visual and oral systems. Having other allied healthcare professionals teach the Physiotherapy and Sports Medicine students resulted in giving the students, who are future allied healthcare professionals, a deeper understanding of the possible effects of head injury on the auditory, vestibular, oral and visual systems. It also gave them more of an awareness of the role of these other professionals and how and when these professionals can help in the patient pathway for head injury patients. This example is discussed in more detail later in this chapter. One may argue that by introducing teaching from other allied healthcare professionals at the stage of education and training is optimum as it encourages trainees from an early stage in their profession to understand, appreciate and be aware of the roles that other professionals can play in the patient care pathway.

In order to enhance cross-professional collaborative practice in healthcare training, there needs to be more innovative strategies devised, these must be developed and implemented [6]. One such strategy to help promote more collaborative practice is by introducing more multidisciplinary, team-based learning activities [6]. These can help promote effective communication, increase teamwork and critical thinking skills [6].

The authors pose that increased multi-professional collaboration across education would be possible if embedded at early educational design stages at the programme and curriculum development stages of setting up new programmes or at programme review stages of existing programmes. This could be achieved in a variety of different ways: one mechanism would be when designing new programmes or reviewing existing programmes to consider if there are any modules which overlap across professions and would benefit from being taught by multiple educators of different professions. To some extent this is sometimes already executed particularly in larger universities for generic subject areas, which allows students from different programmes the opportunity to engage with each other, and also has other added benefits of reducing staffing needs and costs. Often though, a singular lecturer may be in charge of the generic subject as opposed to there being an actual MDT approach to teaching.

Another point of introducing multi-disciplinary teaching and learning could be later in the design process at modular level when designing individual modules or reviewing them. The level of cross collaboration could vary dependent on the subject and scope for collaboration. At a minimal level this could be something similar to the example above where Audiology, Optometry and Dentistry academic staff lectured Physiotherapy and Sports Medicine students. However, it would be more beneficial if this was at a much more enhanced deeper level. For example, when designing the module, academics from these different professions could converge and all be involved in the module design. They could design the module in a way that could be relevant to multiple professions and allow multiple student groups to be taught together. This MDT approach would mean that the training itself was tailored to work for multiple groups of students who would benefit from becoming more aware of the roles of professions other than their own and understanding how they could work together with these professions. This type of MDT in module design would have the added advantage of reduced staffing and costs in the mid to long term. Nevertheless, there are a number of envisaged constraints of trying to introduce multi-disciplinary teaching and learning strategies in the design stages including: the practicality, for example, different programmes develop and have reviews at different stages so the timelines which may suit one profession well may not be ideal for all other professions; most allied healthcare professions are accredited by their individual regulatory bodies which have stringent requirements and the priority of meeting these requirements would typically supersede other needs such as MDT needs; such programmes nowadays can be delivered in different modes of delivery so one group of students from one profession may be taught face-to-face when others are taught online- so there may be a mis-match in mode of delivery requirements and scheduling needs; such programmes often incorporate a placement or work-based learning element and again these schedules may be different across subjects.

3.1 Third level education examples promoting cross professional collaboration

3.1.1 Reflection on a module on concussion and the opportunity to involve other professions

This reflection is set in the context of a three-day block taught module that is delivered within a MSc Sports Medicine programme at a university in the UK. The 20-credit module 'Concussion, Head and Neck Injuries in Sport' was initially included within the MSc Sports Medicine programme as the prevalence of concussive injuries are increasingly being recorded within sport [7]. At the time of module delivery (May 2022), the Consensus Statement from the Berlin 2016 International Conference on Concussion in Sport [7] was the most current recognised guidance on concussion management, and it refers to the '11 Rs' of sports related concussion (recognise, reduce, remove, refer, re-evaluate, rest, rehabilitate, recover, return-to-learn/return-to-sport, reconsider and residual effects). The content of the module had to reflect these aspects within its learning outcomes, delivery content and assessment as part of constructive alignment [8].

To be able to achieve the module learning outcomes and cover the '11Rs', internal and external guest speakers to the university were invited to deliver sessions as outlined in **Figure 1**. In addition to the delivery content, assessments were held the following week to assess students learning from the module with a reactive practical demonstration to a case study and a viva oral examination. These two assessment methods were chosen to assess practical skill demonstration with clinical reasoning (practical demonstration) and to assess wider knowledge around specific subject

Session	Monday 15/05/22	Tuesday 16/05/22	Wednesday 17/05/22	Thursday 18/05/22	Friday 19/05/22
9.00am – 11.00am	Concussion, head and neck injuries: Basic science and anatomy	Practical pitch side assessment and management of head and neck injuries	Research in concussion and future management	Independent study	Independent study
		Break			
11.30am – 1.30pm	Management, rehabilitation and return to play	C-spine extrication	Exam preparation		
		Lunch			
2.00pm – 4.00pm	Dental Injuries	Treatment room assessment of head and neck injuries	Complications of head injury in sport		

Figure 1.
Initial management of concussion, head and neck injuries in sport module content and delivery timetable academic year 2021–2022.

areas taught on the module (viva). The inclusion of both assessment types would reflect and promote Vygotsky's structural learning theory [9] (practical demonstration) and Paiget's cognitive development theory [10] (viva).

Once the module was completed, feedback from educators and students indicated that the dental injuries talk was very interesting as it provided wider learning and taught additional acute pitch side management skills to that of conventional concussion, head and neck pitch side management. These skills would include tooth avulsion management with immediate re-implantation or tooth storage advice for subsequent re-implantation in clinical dental settings. The session also discussed the wider MDT members that could be required if an athlete was subjected to facial injuries and required dental or maxillofacial input. This would have extended the perception of MDT members within Sports Medicine when supporting athletes.

This feedback led to a discussion within the academic postgraduate medical team on how the programme team could further improve the 'Management of Concussion, Head and Neck Injuries in Sport' module with crossover from other departments of the medical school. It was discussed how the sport concussion assessment tool 5th edition (SCAT5) included questions around vestibular and vestibular-ocular symptoms but did not directly assess with relevant tests or provide reasoning for why such symptom questions are included. Therefore, knowledge around visual and audiological impairments as a result of concussive type injuries, would provide deeper knowledge opportunities to the students supporting the pedagogical approach of deep learning [11].

3.1.2 Enhancing cross collaboration in the delivery of head injury/concussion module

When designing the module for the subsequent year, the programme team decided to include sessions on 'concussion and visual impairment' and 'concussion and audiology' to incorporate knowledge around the audio-vestibular and vestibular-ocular systems as discussed previously. The programme team also added a session on 'review and critique of latest guidelines' as a considerable amount of literature was being published from the International Concussion in Sport Conference held in Amsterdam 2022, which would feed into the release of the Amsterdam Consensus Statement and new SCAT 6th edition [12]. New evidence [13] suggested that athletes with delayed concussion symptoms of dizziness and balance problems for 10 days or greater, should receive vestibular rehabilitation to reduce symptoms and aid return to sport. This recommendation was added to the Amsterdam Consensus Statement [12] which was later released. The updated block module was scheduled as in **Figure 2**, to include the additional sessions.

During preparations of the teaching materials for the delivery of the visual and audiology sessions, one of the barriers encountered was presenting the knowledge at the correct level for healthcare professionals who had little prior knowledge of these subject areas. Although students were masters level students, the content had to start at a basic level, then progress into making links to concussion pathology and understanding how symptoms present the way they do. By using Bloom's taxonomic ordering of cognitive skills [14], students would firstly start off with remember and understanding of basic eye and ear anatomy and physiology. Later in the session they would then translate that knowledge into interpretation of light and sound changes with concussion pathophysiology, and how visual and audiological pathologies can occur with direct and indirect blows to the head. These links would challenge student learning with the upper orders of Bloom's taxonomic levels of apply, analyse and evaluate [14] over a very short time span. It was decided by the teaching team that to

Session	Monday 15/05/23	Tuesday 16/05/23	Wednesday 17/05/23	Thursday 18/05/23	Friday 19/05/23
9.00am – 11.00am	Independent study	Concussion, head and neck injuries: Basic science and anatomy	Practical pitch side assessment and management of head and neck injuries	Research in concussion and future management	Dental Injuries
Break					
11.30am – 1.30pm		Management, rehabilitation and return to play	C-spine extrication	Concussion and visual impairment	Concussion and audiology
Lunch					
2.00pm – 4.00pm		Review and critique of latest guidelines	Treatment room assessment of head and neck injuries	Complications of head injury in sport	Exam preparation

Figure 2.
Updated management of concussion, head and neck injuries in sport module content and delivery timetable academic year 2022–2023.

be most effective, less content would achieve more understanding and application of the knowledge.

Another challenge observed within the session was the lack of pre-reading students had completed due to the compacted schedule of the block taught module with the additional sessions. Student feedback reported that although content was good and applicable, students had far too much content delivered within a short period of time, limiting their ability to pre-read before sessions and process teaching content once delivered. The use of block delivery modules supports a 'block and blend' approach where immersive scheduling provides face-to-face activity-based learning alongside blended learning of online learning materials [15]. Students may not have been familiar with this style of delivery, but the additional sessions from last year did make the schedule more concentrated. To support students, the assessments were held one week later than the previous year to allow students more time to prepare and drop-in revision sessions were timetabled to allow further support if needed.

As students completed the block taught module, an appreciation of visual and audiological pathologies in relation to concussion onset was established as evidenced in their viva assessment. Specific questioning around vestibulo-ocular symptoms allowed students to demonstrate their understanding and show links to the anatomy they had learned. Students also had the opportunity to discuss visual and audiological pathologies that would require referral following recognition of their signs and symptoms. This achieved the goal of widening the MDT approach with concussion management and allowed further understanding of the symptom checklist used in the SCAT 6th edition.

3.1.3 Digital devices, vision and ergonomics: the collaborative role of Optometrists and Musculoskeletal clinicians in digital vision

The current ways in which people use their vision and eyes has changed faster that the visual system is evolving. This means that Optometrists are having to provide care to patients whose daily living demands are greater than what the eyes and the body can cope with. One of the main changes has been in the use of digital devices which are electronic units that can send, receive, generate, and display communications [16] Access to internet and digital devices has changed the way in which we interact with each other and our work-life. There has been nearly 50% increase of internet users since 2005 [17].

Between 1992 to 2000, the percentage of workers using a computer all the time at work increased from 7.6% to 11.9% [18]. It appears that before the 2000s, most of the digital device use was in workplaces [18]. As the years progressed, use of digital devices became more common place in social situations as well as the workplace. Since the Covid-19 pandemic, there has been increase in digital device use in education [18]. Globally, in 2023 79% of 'youth' compared to 65% of the 'rest of the population' use the internet [19]. The term 'Youth' is referring to people between 15 and 25 years of age who use the internet as a percentage of the total population aged between 15 and 25, the 'rest of the population' is referring to and includes all people under 15 or over 24 years old [19].

In addition to the shift from a typical working age group using digital devices to broader age groups, which includes school aged children, the traditional display screen equipment (DSE) or visual display units (VDUs) have been replaced with more mobile units. There has been a shift from just using the static (desktop computers) or hand-held devices (tablets or mobiles) to wearable devices such as smart watches, smart home devices or smart glasses [17].

The following are the potential impacts on how Optometrists care for their patients:

Ergonomics and posture

The advice on setting up a workstation has been based on the traditional desktop computers where the patient's eyes need to be 50–70 cm from the screen, the top of the screen needs to be at eye level and the arms need to be straight when using the keyboard. This set-up ensures that patients' eyes can focus (accommodate) comfortably for the distance that the screen was set. The visual system (eyes) will need between 1.5 dioptres to 2.0 dioptres to focus on a target which is set at 50–70 cm. It has been theorised that to reduce overstrain of the visual system, one third of the patient's accommodative/focus power needs to remain in reserve [20]. It was this theory which has been used to set out the workstation requirements and the continued clinical advice that Optometrists give their patients in terms of digital screen use related eye strain. The alignment of the screen to the eyes is based on the posture of the spine and the angle of the arms to the keyboard. In relation to the ergonomics of the desk and chair.

As the Global Overview 2023 report [17] indicates, the use of traditional desktop computers is falling, and most people will have a set up where they are looking at a laptop on a desk as well as looking at a held-held device such as a smartphone or a tablet. This means that the viewing distance for the held-held device is around 40 cm away from the eyes whilst the laptop screen is around 55 cm away. The laptop screen is usually closer than the static desktop monitor as the keyboard is attached to the screen on a laptop. This means that when someone is using a laptop, they need to arrange their arms in a comfortable position to allow them to type using the attached keyboard making the viewing distance of the screen closer. The position of the screen is below eye level and patients have to bend their heads downwards and maintaining this position for a prolong period of time can cause muscular strain in the neck and the base of the head.

As the viewing distances of mobile phones and tablet is much closer to a viewing distance with a computer screen, the constant moving of focus between these different distances throughout the day can cause eye strain. Visual fatigue in VDU users has been reported for many years [21] and this has since been renamed as Digital Eye Strain (DES). A recent review in 2022 showed that the prevalence of DES in children rose to 50–60% [22]. The review discussed management options to reduce the symptoms of DES but it only considered the role of the eye care practitioner rather than looking at it holistically.

Optometrists regularly hear patients report both symptoms of DES and an increase in neck and back ache, therefore the advice given by Optometrists to their patients' needs to include guidance about good musculoskeletal health. 47% of computers users have complained of low back pain after three to four hours of use [23]. This means that there is a need for Optometrists and Musculoskeletal specialists to collaborate when advising patients on good habits around digital device use to ensure that patients do not experience prolonged/sustained problems which can affect the quality of life. Setting up an optometry programme within a university's medical school, meant that Optometry staff had the opportunity to deliver a programme with input from different disciplines such as Musculoskeletal specialists.

Outside of the academic setting and multi-disciplinary teaching of clinicians, the importance of these professions working together can be seen in the 2023 "Love Your Eyes at Work" World Sight Day campaign by the International Agency for the Prevention of Blindness where a poster which indicates 6 ways to reduce eyestrain mentions ergonomics [24].

The posture of Optometrists

As digital devices become part of everyday life, they are also changing the work environment of Optometrists. Due to the strange sitting positions that Optometrists need to work, and the repeated nature of these tasks, there is a history of complaints of back pain amongst these professionals [25]. Optometrists must be sat to one side of the patient but be able to stretch to reach across the patients' eyes, stand over the patient to look into the eye to assess the health of the eye and to swing machinery around to bring it in front of and away from the patients, and this is typically repeated many times a day for each patient.

In addition to the existing musculoskeletal issues, the digital screen use within the consulting rooms has increased – vision testing charts are now often either LCD screens or computer screens, often nowadays, record cards are computerised, and referrals are electronic. This means that alongside the usual awkward positions that an Optometrist has to adopt to assess a patient's eyes, compounding this they now have to use digital devices on a daily basis. Most digital devices are added to the consulting rooms after the clinical equipment has been installed and therefore the working distances and set-up required for use of computers is not followed making it an uncomfortable working environment.

In the authors' current university, as part of the training of Optometry students, students are taught about digital eye strain and posture recommendations for their own self-care. This is to reduce the risk of musculoskeletal pain in terms of the postures the students need to adopt to carry out specific clinical tests using the guidance/advice from Physiotherapy lecturers. This is the same advice that Optometrists offer patients about digital eye strain. A few years ago, an ergonomic specialist sat in for a day to observe Optometrists in their work environment and the ergonomic specialist provided some stances and sitting positions which would reduce the strain. These stances and positions are now included in the clinical skills teaching of Optometry students at the university and represents a positive impact of a multi-disciplinary working.

The involvement of eye care (Optometrists, Dispensing Opticians, Ophthalmologists and Orthoptists) and Musculoskeletal professionals is intertwined, and thus the there is a need to further explore the collaborative working partnership between these two disciplines. As technology changes and how people work and live is constantly evolving, multidisciplinary working is going to be paramount for offering quality care to patients.

3.1.4 Further opportunities for enhanced cross collaboration approaches in healthcare and higher education

Working within a multi-disciplinary setting within the university has the benefit of giving staff the opportunity to learn from other professions; an example for Optometry staff is the learning from colleagues within the Physiotherapy and Sports Medicine courses. This collaboration has had a positive impact as when teaching Optometry students about prescribing for DES/VDU users in the sub-topic of occupational Optometry, the ergonomic advice and good posture guidance is taught alongside the optical theories. It is envisaged that this initial exchange of specialist experiences and learning will be developed into an interprofessional module where Optometry, Ophthalmic Dispensing and Physiotherapy students can be taught about digital eye strain and ergonomics. As discussed earlier, there is already a unit within the Concussion module where a multi-disciplinary approach between Optometry, Audiology, Dentistry, and Sports Medicine is being utilised for teaching students. Continued collaboration is planned in this area with the planning to grow the joint teaching sessions in several different programmes.

Due to the ageing population, the incidence of falls is increasing. Falls are one of the most common problems in older adults [26]. The prevention and management of falls is a global challenge [27]. Managing patients with falls is another area where the authors of the current chapter feel there is scope to cross collaborate across their three respective professions to help better manage patients with falls. Policymakers and healthcare providers need to seriously consider and focus on both prevention of falls and intervention [26]. Simple changes can help reduce the risk falls including; providing assistive equipment, proper lighting within homes, regular eye examinations in the elderly, and proper footwear [26]. This type of prevention would require a MDT including Physiotherapists, Social Workers, Optometrists and Podiatrists. Whilst prevention is key, for those who do have falls, diagnosis and intervention and rehabilitation can significantly impact the quality of life of an individual. Audio-vestibular Physicians, Audiologists and Physiotherapists can work together in the diagnosis and rehabilitation of those with vestibular problems who may have had falls or are at risk of falling. As discussed in the example earlier in the chapter in an educational setting there has been some cross professional teaching in this area. However, there are many more opportunities for this to evolve in the future whereby at the next programme review Medical, Audiological and Physiotherapy professional academics could consider how they could teach and design these modules together. In the healthcare setting, for patients with problems in the balance system, there is a lot of cross-over work between the professions particularly in the rehabilitation of these patients, therefore it would be advantageous to consider the elements of training of some elements for these professions together. Falls is just one example where the authors of this current chapter and their respective professions could collaborate.

There are many other areas in ageing where MDT would enhance care of this population. For example, one particularly challenging area is cardiovascular disease. It accounts for 17,500 deaths globally and this represents nearly half of all non-communicable disease (NCD) deaths [28]. Jennings poses that it the collaboration between multiple professionals including Physicians, Nurses, Pharmacists, Psychologists and other allied healthcare professionals which will help to win the battle against NCDs [28].

Alzheimer's Disease (AD) is another common occurrence in the older population. AD is the most common form of dementia affecting the ageing population [29, 30].

The eye has been shown to be an early biomarker for AD [29, 30]. There is also an indication that there are links between dementia and hearing loss [31, 32] and that Presbyacusis (age-related hearing loss) can be an indicator for dementia [31]. Although a lot more research is needed to get a consensus on the association between hearing loss and dementia, it is clear that it would be advantageous if there was more collaboration amongst Audiology, Optometry and other professions in the patient pathway for patients with dementia. Multidisciplinary approaches adopted for AD so far have made substantial contributions in helping to understand both the cognitive and physiological changes associated with it [33].

4. Opportunities and barriers to MDT within healthcare settings

Huddles are short briefings which are designed to give healthcare staff opportunities to meet, they help professionals to stay informed, evaluate things that have happened, and make plans which helps to result in well-coordinated patient care [34]. A systematic review in 2021 has demonstrated that daily multi-disciplinary huddles can help improve both teamwork and healthcare professionals' job satisfaction [35]. Collegiality is important for both staff and patients [35]. Multidisciplinary huddles can help teams to address issues such as safety concerns and staffing issues [35]. Huddles are a mechanism to look at an individual patient's goals of care collaboratively [35]. Introducing daily multidisciplinary huddles into healthcare are an opportunity to increase collaboration amongst professionals. However, often time constraints and increasing waiting lists can make this difficult. Therefore, even if daily huddles are difficult to schedule, weekly huddles may be another option, which could help facilitate more MDT.

Other barriers to MDT in healthcare settings are typically: financial constraints; lack of flexibility in systems; reluctance to collaborate; hierarchical systems; time constraints; having a designated organisational lead to arrange MDT meetings/huddles; logistical issues such as a mis-match in different professionals' rotas; adversity to change; and a lack of motivation as MDT set-up may require time in the initial stages. Therefore, the authors pose the question that in order to overcome/address some of these challenges, whether MDT should be incorporated at a higher strategic management stage of healthcare organisations as a target/goal so that when this filters down into individual departments, it is easier to accommodate MDT and in turn MDT becomes the "normal" way of working? Therefore, there needs to be a shift or movement towards prioritising MDT in healthcare settings. The collaboration between specialisms and reducing "silo" working should be encouraged from the top of organisation down to those working "on the ground" directly with or for patients. Having this "buy-in" from higher up would help create protected MDT times which would overcome one of the main current barriers to collaboration.

5. Opportunities and barriers to cross professional collaboration in higher educational settings

The authors believe that with the ever changing and demanding healthcare environments, that the education of allied healthcare students could be further enhanced and modernised in order to help meet the growing and challenging workforce needs. As discussed earlier, for many years often generic transversal skills have often been taught in universities to multiple groups of students in the same session. However, there are many more opportunities to develop and increase the level of MDT between academics teaching different healthcare subjects. One such way is to introduce modules on "hot" topics such as ageing, one such example may be a module on Multidisciplinary Approaches to Ageing Processes. This type of module could be designed and taught by MDT and would benefit the students' training. Additionally, by gaining this training from different professionals will aid trainees in the future, as by the time they become graduates they will already have seen how to work as part of teams across disciplines. It will make them more aware from an early stage of training/career how other professionals contribute to a patient's care pathway. The authors envisage that one of the main challenges would be accommodating such modules in often already tight time constraints of a programme delivery. This type of module would work well for primary training of healthcare students, the level of this primary training can differ, in some professions it may be at foundation level, in others at bachelors level or other healthcare training is at masters level.

The collaboration within the professions mentioned is slowly developing for students studying these disciplines but there is scope to develop a further range of continuous professional development (CPD) courses for clinicians who are already providing care for their patients. One such example as discussed earlier is the growth of the use of digital devices which is on an exponential growth and the prevalence of digital eye strain and musculoskeletal issues will increase. In the near future combined clinics where a patient can have an eye examination as well as a physiotherapy appointment with a combined management plan is a strong possibility.

CPD is a key lifelong component of a healthcare professionals working life. Micro-credentials are a key mechanism to support ongoing CPD for the busy healthcare professional. The impact of the acceleration of online learning post the Covid-19 pandemic has widened a world of training opportunities including the increased volume of micro-credentials available or employees wishing to enrol on CPD courses [36]. Having short courses available online makes CPD training more accessible and with an ever-increasing international focus on both population health and public health, it is timely to start to widen the CPD opportunities for healthcare professionals. As well as having subject specific short CPD courses, there is a potential growth for more generic multidisciplinary modules that would be attractive to different healthcare professionals, modules could be around evolving areas such as: Multidisciplinary Challenges and Complexity of Healthcare Provision for Older Adults; Innovation in Support of Active and Healthy Ageing; and Innovation in Healthcare Technologies. These suggestions are all topics which are emerging and of use to the modern allied healthcare professional.

6. Conclusion

It is evident that the future of healthcare and meeting ever complex healthcare needs is a continuing global challenge. However, the authors pose that more MDT working may help alleviate some of the current burdens and challenges on health services. More strategic and streamlined processes encouraging MDT are needed. There are also many new and current developments which may further assist/ support healthcare challenges. Modern technological developments and innovations may complement implementation of multidisciplinary approaches. One such development which may be used to positively contribute to more streamlined healthcare processes is Artificial Intelligence (AI) [37]. Sezgin poses that AI is creating a paradigm shift in healthcare by complementing and enhancing the skills of medical and healthcare professional [37]. In addition, to increasing MDT in the healthcare setting, it is crucial to look at opportunities to increase more MDT in the training of future allied healthcare professionals. In order for this MDT to be effective, it is better to incorporate this at a higher early stage of programme design and module design in higher education so that MDT is not just an "add-on" or "after thought", but instead an overarching ethos of all allied healthcare programmes and in turn all healthcare professionals of the future.

Author details

Kirpa Chandan*, Russell Hitchen and Rupal Lovell-Patel
University of Central Lancashire, Preston, United Kingdom

*Address all correspondence to: kchandan@uclan.ac.uk

References

[1] World Health Organisation (WHO). [Internet]. 2024. Available from: https://www.who.int/teams/integrated-health-services/clinical-services-and-systems/service-organizations-and-integration [Accessed: March 18, 2024]

[2] Gola M, Brambilla A, Barach P, Signorelli C, Capolongo S. Educational challenges in healthcare design: Training multidisciplinary professionals for future hospitals and healthcare. Annals of Hygiene Preventive and Community Medicine. 2020;**32**(5):549-566. DOI: 10.7416/ai.2020.2375

[3] National Health Service (NHS). [Internet]. 2022. Available from: https://transform.england.nhs.uk/information-governance/guidance/information-governance-guidance-support-multidisciplinary-teams-mdts/ [Accessed: March 17, 2024]

[4] Leeftink G, Bikker IA, Vliegen IMH, Boucherie RJ. Multi-disciplinary planning in health care: A review. Health Systems. 2020;**9**(2):95-118. DOI: 10.1080/20476965.2018.1436909

[5] Benagiano G, Brosens I. The multidisciplinary approach. Best Practice & Research Clinical Obstetrics & Gynaecology. 2014;**28**(8):1114-1122. DOI: 10.1016/j.bpobgyn.2014.08.006

[6] Masters C, Baker VO, Jodon H. Multidisciplinary, team-based learning: The simulated interdisciplinary to multidisciplinary progressive-level education (SIMPLE©) approach. Clinical Simulation in Nursing. 2013;**9**(5):e171-e178. DOI: 10.1016/j.ecns.2011.11.007

[7] McCrory P, Meeuwisse W, Dvorak J, Aubry M, Bailes J, Broglio S, et al. Consensus statement on concussion in sport – the 5th international conference on concussion in sport held in Berlin October 2016. British Journal of Sports Medicine. 2017;**51**:838-847. DOI: 10.1136/bjsports-2017-097699

[8] Biggs J. Enhancing teaching through constructive alignment. Higher Education. 1996;**32**:347-364

[9] Newman S, Latifi A. Vygotsky, education, and teacher education. Journal of Education for Teaching. 2021;**47**(1):4-17

[10] Ikiugu M. Chapter 3 – psychological theories that have contributed to the development of occupational therapy practice. In: Psychosocial Conceptual Practice Models in Occupational Therapy. Mosby: Elsevier; 2007. pp. 41-74

[11] Warburton K. Deep learning and education for sustainability. International Journal of Sustainability in Higher Education. 2003;**4**(1):44-56

[12] Patricios JS, Schneider KJ, Dvorak J, Ahmed OH, Blauwet C, Cantu RC, et al. Consensus statement on concussion in sport: the 6th International Conference on Concussion in Sport–Amsterdam, October 2022. British Journal of Sports Medicine. 2023;**57**:695-711

[13] Schneider K, Schneider KJ, Critchley ML, Anderson V, Davis GA, Debert CT, et al. Targeted interventions and their effect on recovery in children, adolescents, and adults who have suffered a sport-related concussion: A systematic review. British Journal of Sports Medicine. 2023;**57**(12):771-779

[14] Adams N. Bloom's taxonomy of cognitive learning objectives. Journal

of the Medical Library Association. 2015;**103**(3):152-153

[15] Buck E, Tyrrell K. Block and blend: A mixed method investigation into the impact of a pilot block teaching and blended learning approach upon student outcomes and experience. Journal of Further and Higher Education. 2022;**46**(8):1078-1091

[16] Law Insider. Digital Device Definition. [Internet]. Available from: https://www.lawinsider.com/dictionary/digital-device [Accessed: March 17, 2024]

[17] Data Reportal. Global Internet User Overview [Internet]. 2023. Available from: https://datareportal.com/reports/digital-2023-global-overview-report [Accessed: March 01, 2024]

[18] Andries F, Smulders P, Dhondt S. The use of computers among the workers in the European Union and its impact on the quality of work. Behaviour & IT. 2002;**21**:441-447

[19] ITU. Youth Internet use Facts and Figures 2023 [Internet]. 2023. Available from: https://www.itu.int/itu-d/reports/statistics/2023/10/10/ff23-youth-internet-use/ [Accessed: March 18, 2024]

[20] Millodot M, Millodot S. Presbyopia correction and the accommodation in reserve. Ophthalmic and Physiological Optics. 1989;**9**:126-132

[21] Dain SJ, McCarthy AK, Chan-Ling T. Symptoms in VDU operators. American Journal of Optometry and Physiological Optics. 1988;**65**(3):162-167

[22] Kaur K, Gurnani B, Nayak S, Deori N, Kaur S, Jethani J, et al. Digital eye strain- a comprehensive review. Ophthalmology and Therapy. 2022;**11**(5):1655-1680

[23] Borhany T, Shahid E, Siddique WA, Ali H. Musculoskeletal problems in frequent computer and internet users. Journal of Family Medicine and Primary Care. 2018;**7**(2):337-339

[24] IAPB. Work Pack – 6 ways to Reduce Eyestrain (iapb.org). [Internet] 2023. Available from: https://www.iapb.org/wp-content/uploads/2023/07/6-Ways-to-reduce-eyestrain.pdf [Accessed: March 18, 2024]

[25] Al Taisan A, Al Qurainees AE, Al Sowayigh OM, Al Owayfir MA. Musculoskeletal pain among eye care professionals. Cureus. 2023;**15**(5)

[26] Salari N, Darvishi N, Ahmadipanah M, Shohaimi S, Mohammadi M. Global prevalence of falls in the older adults: A comprehensive systematic review and Meta-analysis. Journal of Orthopaedic Surgery and Research. 2022;**17**:334. DOI: 10.1186/s13018-022-03222-1

[27] Montero-Odasso M, van der Velde N, Martin FC, Petrovic M, Tan MP, Ryg J, et al. The task force on global guidelines for falls in older adults, world guidelines for falls prevention and management for older adults: A global initiative. Age and Ageing. 2022;**51**(9):afac205. DOI: 10.1093/ageing/afac205

[28] Jennings C, Astin F. A multidisciplinary approach to prevention. European journal of. Preventive Cardiology. 2017;**24**(suppl. 3):77-87. DOI: 10.1177/2047487317709118

[29] Javaid FZ, Brenton J, Guo L, Cordeiro MF. Visual and ocular manifestations of Alzheimer's disease and their use as biomarkers for diagnosis and progression. Frontiers in Neurology. 2016;**7**(55):1-11. DOI: 10.3389/fneur.2016.00055

[30] Lim JKH, Li Q-X, He Z, Vingrys AJ, Wong VHY, Currier N, et al. The eye as a biomarker for Alzheimer's disease. Frontiers in Neuroscience. 2016;**10**:536. DOI: 10.3389/fnins.2016.00536

[31] Chern A, Golub JS. Age-related hearing loss and dementia. Alzheimer Disease and Associated Disorders. 2019;**33**(3):285-290. DOI: 10.1097/WAD.0000000000000325

[32] Liang Z, Li A, Xu Y, Qian X, Gao X. Hearing loss and dementia: A Meta-analysis of prospective cohort studies. Frontiers in Aging Neuroscience. 2021;**13**:695117. DOI: 10.3389/fnagi.2021.695117

[33] Ellis KA, Rainey-Smith SR, Rembach A, Lance Macaulay S, Villemagne VL, AIBL research group. Enabling a multidisciplinary approach to the study of ageing and Alzheimer's disease: An update from the Australian imaging biomarkers and lifestyle (AIBL) study. International Review of Psychiatry. 2013;**25**(6):699-710. DOI: 10.3109/09540261.2013.870136

[34] Goldenhar LM, Brady PW, Sutcliffe KM, Muething SE. Huddling for high reliability and situation awareness. British Medical Journal Quality and Safety. 2013;**22**(11):899-906. DOI: 10.1136/bmjqs-2012-001467

[35] Rowan BL, Anjara S, De Brún A, MacDonalD S, Kearns EC, Marnane N, et al. The impact of huddles on a multidisciplinary healthcare Teams' work engagement, teamwork and job satisfaction: A systematic review. Journal of Evaluation in Clinical Practice. 2022;**28**:382-393. DOI: 10.1111/jep.13648

[36] Chandan K, Kealey C, Timpson P, Murphy B. Experience-based reflections on the blended learning pedagogical approach in higher education. In: Waller L, Waller S, editors. Higher Education - Reflections from the Field – Volume 3 [Internet]. Education and Human Development. London, UK, London, UK: IntechOpen; 2023. DOI: 10.5772/intechopen.112127

[37] Sezgin E. Artificial intelligence in healthcare: Complementing, not replacing, doctors and healthcare providers. Digital Health. 2023;**9**:1-5. DOI: 10.1177/20552076231186520